A LETTER FROM PETER MUNK

Since we started the Munk Debates, my wife, Melanie, and I have been deeply gratified at how quickly they have captured the public's imagination. From the time of our first event in May 2008, we have hosted what I believe are some of the most exciting public policy debates in Canada and internationally. Global in focus, the Munk Debates have tackled a range of issues, such as humanitarian intervention, the effectiveness of foreign aid, the threat of global warming, religion's impact on geopolitics, the rise of China, and the decline of Europe. These compelling topics have served as intellectual and ethical grist for some of the world's most important thinkers and doers, from Henry Kissinger to Tony Blair, Christopher Hitchens to Paul Krugman, Peter Mandelson to Fareed Zakaria.

The issues raised at the Munk Debates have not only fostered public awareness, but they have also helped many of us become more involved and, therefore, less intimidated by the concept of globalization. It is so easy to be inward-looking. It is so easy to be xenophobic. It is so easy to be nationalistic. It is hard to go into the unknown. Globalization, for many people, is an abstract concept at best. The purpose of this debate series is to help people feel more familiar with our fast-changing world and more comfortable participating in the universal dialogue about the issues and events that will shape our collective future.

I don't need to tell you that there are many, many burning issues. Global warming, the plight of extreme poverty, genocide, our shaky financial order: these are just a few of the critical issues that matter to people. And it seems to me, and to my foundation board members, that the quality of the public dialogue on these critical issues diminishes in direct proportion to the salience and number of these issues clamouring for our attention. By trying to highlight the most important issues at crucial moments in the global conversation, these debates not only profile the ideas and opinions of some of the world's brightest thinkers, but they also crystallize public passion and knowledge, helping to tackle some of the challenges confronting humankind.

I have learned in life—and I'm sure many of you will share this view—that challenges bring out the best in us. I hope you'll agree that the participants in these debates challenge not only each other but also each of us to think clearly and logically about important problems facing our world.

Peter Munk (1927–2018)
Founder, Aurea Foundation
Toronto, Ontario

CHINA AND THE WEST

MCMASTER AND PILLSBURY
VS. MAHBUBANI AND WANG

THE MUNK DEBATES

Edited by Rudyard Griffiths

ANANSI

Published in Canada in 2019 and the USA in 2019 by House of Anansi Press Inc.
www.houseofanansi.com

23 22 21 20 19   1 2 3 4 5

Library and Archives Canada Cataloguing in Publication

Title: China and the West : McMaster and Pillsbury vs. Mahbubani and Wang :
the Munk debates / edited by Rudyard Griffiths.
Names: McMaster, H. R., 1962- panelist. | Pillsbury, Michael, panelist. |
Mahbubani, Kishore, panelist. | Wang, Huiyao, panelist. | Griffiths, Rudyard,
editor.
Series: Munk debates.
Description: Series statement: Munk debates
Identifiers: Canadiana (print) 20190137568 | Canadiana (ebook) 20190137673
| ISBN 9781487007188 (softcover) | ISBN 9781487007195 (EPUB) |
ISBN 9781487007201 (Kindle)
Subjects: LCSH: China—Foreign relations—Western countries. | LCSH:
Western countries—Foreign relations—China. | LCSH: China—Foreign
economic relations—Western countries. | LCSH: China—Civilization. | LCSH:
China—Economic conditions. | LCSH: China—Politics and government.
Classification: LCC HF1604.Z4 W47 2019 | DDC 337.510182/1—dc23

Cover design: Alysia Shewchuk
Transcription: Transcript Heroes

 **Canada Council
for the Arts** **Conseil des Arts
du Canada**   **ONTARIO ARTS COUNCIL
CONSEIL DES ARTS DE L'ONTARIO**
an Ontario government agency
un organisme du gouvernement de l'Ontario

*We acknowledge for their financial support of our publishing program the Canada
Council for the Arts, the Ontario Arts Council, and the Government of Canada.*

Printed and bound in Canada

MIX
Paper from
responsible sources
FSC® C103567

CONTENTS

Pre-Debate Interviews with Moderator Rudyard Griffiths

H. R. MCMASTER IN CONVERSATION
WITH RUDYARD GRIFFITHS

RUDYARD GRIFFITHS: General McMaster, thank you for coming to Toronto to be part of this debate. We're really looking forward to your words tonight.

H. R. MCMASTER: Thanks, Rudyard. It's a real privilege to be here. I'm looking forward to it.

RUDYARD GRIFFITHS: It's a privilege to host you. Let's jump right in here and talk a little bit about your overall view of China and its role in the world today. It's interesting that you see this conflict as not necessarily just about economics; you think that there's almost an existential dimension to it, that it's a conflict between the democratic world order and a very powerful rising regime that has, in your view, authoritarian characteristics. Explain that for us.

H. R. MCMASTER: I wouldn't say it's an existential conflict. I think it's a competition; it's a competition with the Chinese Communist Party and the policies of that party that aim to stifle any kind of freedom and individual rights within their own society, but also to export that model to other countries in an effort to challenge the international system as it exists and replace it with a new order that's sympathetic to Chinese interests, with China, as President Xi has said, at the centre. In many ways, this is an attempt, I think, to re-establish the tributary system in Chinese dynastic history, in which countries that sign up can enjoy free trade as long as they are in a servile relationship with China. So, I think China poses a significant threat to our free and open societies.

RUDYARD GRIFFITHS: Now, you're going to hear an argument at this debate about who is the biggest beneficiary of the liberal international order, at least over the last several decades. Surely that's China. So why would China threaten a global system that has been so favourable to them in terms of their economic indicators, in terms of the health of the society that they've created?

H. R. MCMASTER: Right. It's important to remember that the Cultural Revolution that Mao used to purge the party really destroyed the Chinese economy. Their economy in the 1980s was a basket case. So, it was really the West, the international order, welcoming China in that helped them have a tremendously successful period of economic growth, lifting 800 million people out of poverty. And the way China did that was to reform. So, there were reasons to be optimistic in the post–Cold War period that China, having been welcomed into the order, would continue to liberalize its economy, and, as it prospered, China would play by the rules and then ultimately liberalize its political system as well.

Well, what's happened is that those economic reforms stalled under Hu Jintao, and they completely went into reverse under Xi Jinping. Last year, 2018, was the first year in which the Chinese private sector did not grow, and it was the first time that the percentage of the Chinese economy that is state-driven grew relative to the private economy. This is because what Xi Jinping is endeavouring to do more than any other objective is tighten the party's exclusive grip on power. And the party sees these structural aspects of the state-driven authoritarian capitalist model as essential to maintaining its grip on power.

RUDYARD GRIFFITHS: Another question that will probably come up in this debate is: Why is America paying attention to this now? I mean, you had the last twenty, thirty years to think through what your China policy should be. It seems to be a hard pivot right now from the more dovish view earlier to something you might describe as hawkish. Why is that happening?

H. R. MCMASTER: I think it's because of the recognition that the assumptions on which previous policies were based are false. I mean, you hosted a great debate here eight years ago on China, and David Li was one of the debaters. In that debate, he said, "Look, we *are* liberalizing," and he gave some examples. He said, "Chinese people can express their opinions now," and he said, "Our young generation won't be satisfied and they're going to demand even more reforms."

Well, that young generation is being brainwashed and brutally repressed by the state's really tight grip on the information that they have access to, then also by the stifling of any kind of ideas or discussions involving concepts like rule of law. If you talk about rule of law and you're a professor or a student, you get arrested. Many of these students were arrested and they disappeared—until they reappeared later in confession videos. Books on rule of law are taken down from university bookshelves and destroyed.

Even with Marxist organizations that were advocating for workers' rights, those universities in which that was happening were raided and the students arrested. So, what's happened is, I think, a broad recognition—not just not in the United States but throughout the world—that China does *not* intend to liberalize. China does not intend to play by the rules and, in fact, wants to break apart the international order and replace it with a new order sympathetic to the Chinese Communist Party. And so what you see in response is sixteen other nations joining Canada in December 2018 in calling out the sustained campaign of industrial espionage against Western companies. What you see is a great deal of co-operation internationally in confronting China's efforts to control the ocean by developing the South China Sea and militarizing the islands. And nobody controls the ocean.

I think this is really one of the few issues in the United States these days that brings both parties together. But there is also, I think, a recognition on the part of our free and open societies, as the European Union just announced last month, that China is advocating a system that would undermine everything we hold dear in terms of universal rights, and free and open and fair and reciprocal trade and economic relations.

RUDYARD GRIFFITHS: A couple of other counter-arguments to try out on you: the first is that some people will posit that the reason America is focusing on this trade issue now is that they realize that China is a technological and economic threat, and so in a sense the United States is trying to create a global alliance to push back against China—not to defend the liberal international order or universal values but to defend America's narrow national interest. Why do you reject that assumption?

H. R. MCMASTER: I reject that because what the Chinese Communist Party is doing is pursuing a strategy that they call military-civil fusion. There is a directive called Document No. 9 that leaked out a few years ago—and if you're Chinese and you even talk about it you get thrown into prison—that essentially revealed the strategy of the Chinese Communist Party, which is to direct an integrated effort across academia, private companies and industries, and the military. What they want to do is to gain global dominance of the emerging economy, and then also apply emerging technologies to military capabilities in a way that allows them to pursue their objectives, which are dangerous to all nations. Those that are on the periphery of China would essentially become vassal states as China endeavours to develop exclusionary areas of influence across the Indo-Pacific region and then challenges the United States and other free and open societies globally.

If you look at who their client states are, it's Venezuela in the Western Hemisphere, it's Zimbabwe in Africa, it's Cambodia on its periphery. These are oppressive regimes, and what you might say is that the Chinese Communist Party is trying to make the world safe for authoritarianism, because that's how they can extend their influence most effectively.

RUDYARD GRIFFITHS: Another argument in this debate is that China can say, "Look, we're actually a good global citizen. We're a member of the Paris Accord. We didn't pull out of that agreement like the United States. You complain obviously about our assertion of territorial rights in the South China Sea, but we're a signatory of the U.N. Law of the Sea. The United States is not." There's a whole series of examples like that, where China seems to be a good multilateral actor, whereas the recent tenor of American engagement with the world seems more unilateralist. How do you respond to that?

H. R. MCMASTER: Well, China actually participates in international fora so that they can undermine those institutions and bend them toward their agenda to achieve this hegemonic influence and put China back at centre stage. So, for example, China was welcomed in 2001 into the World Trade Organization [WTO] and pledged to liberalize its economy, to stop state subsidies to state-owned enterprises, and to stop the forced transfer of intellectual property just for the privilege of doing business in their economy. They didn't make good on *any* of those promises. Also, even though the United States is not a signatory to the Law of the Sea in terms of freedom of navigation and so forth, the U.S. adheres to it and is a good international participant and enforcer of international law. China is breaking that law every day in continued reclamation efforts and militarization in the South China Sea.

Also, I think that what China is doing with the Paris Accord, for one example, is portraying their behaviour as supportive of the international order even as they undermine these efforts. China is poisoning the global environment even as they adhere to an agreement that's pretty flawed. The problem with the Paris Accord is that it gave us a false sense of security. It didn't really address the world's biggest polluters — India and others, but mainly China. And China, under the Belt and Road Initiative, is exporting 260 coal-fired plants to places like South Africa and Kenya. They're trying to appear as if they're a good citizen while they're actually undermining the system.

RUDYARD GRIFFITHS: This is obviously a very personal issue for you, and I'm wondering why you've chosen to speak out about it. Was there something that happened in your career? Were you previously part of that other foreign policy establishment that thought, "Oh, look, China's not a threat; they'll reform," and then you had an epiphany? Or was it your experience in the White House that led you to this firm set of beliefs?

H. R. MCMASTER: The vast majority of my career was spent in Europe and in the Middle East and Central Asia. Of course, China always figures prominently across the world. And I had been a student of Chinese history; I taught it as part of our survey course at West Point. But I really didn't focus on China very much until I came into the job as national security advisor. One of the important aspects of that job, I think, is to examine existing policies and challenge the assumptions on which those policies are based.

Once we took a look at the old policy of strategic engagement with China and identified that it was underpinned by this really implicit and demonstrably false assumption that China would behave in a way that's supportive of the international order, we recognized that we really needed a shift. We needed to move toward a policy that acknowledged that we are in a competition with an authoritarian closed system that is not only repressing its own people but also exporting its model to other regimes.

So, after recognizing the need to compete with China, we thought the best way forward was to have a conversation with the Chinese Communist Party and say, "This is not in your interest to behave this way," and to get off the path that could lead to confrontation. Because China had gone unchallenged for so long, it was becoming more and more aggressive, and so this strategy of competition, rather than just engagement under the belief that China would liberalize, was appropriate.

I think what you're seeing is the adoption of that approach across the world. Within the European Union and throughout North America, our friends in the Western Hemisphere are very concerned about, for example, the effect of the Chinese debt trap that they use to try to co-opt and then coerce countries into supporting Chinese foreign policy.

Ecuador is a great example. They built a $2.6 billion dam in a lake at the base of an active volcano. The turbines in this dam are clogged with silt and trees. The first time it was fired up it blew out the whole electrical system in the country; it already had cracks in it! Of course, what China has done with this sort of predatory economic strategy that they're implementing is that, in exchange for building this dam, and for Ecuador to service the debt associated with it, China now takes 80 percent of Ecuador's oil exports at a discount and resells it on the international market.

Look at Venezuela. China is making money on the backs of the starving Venezuelan people. And they're doing that by propping up Nicolás Maduro with continued cash flow while Maduro now sells almost all of Venezuela's oil to the Chinese, who don't use any of it but just sell it internationally at a markup. China is profiting while the Venezuelan people starve. And so, this has tremendous non-partisan support, not just from the United States or the Republican Party: the recognition that we have to really confront this pernicious danger to our free and open societies.

MICHAEL PILLSBURY IN CONVERSATION
WITH RUDYARD GRIFFITHS

RUDYARD GRIFFITHS: Michael, having read your book *The Hundred-Year Marathon*, which I greatly enjoyed, the question I want to start with is: What was the moment or the event that caused you to really rethink some of your most basic assumptions about China? You're an especially interesting thinker on this topic because you're someone who has made an intellectual journey. You started at one place and you've ended up somewhere very different. Why did that happen?

MICHAEL PILLSBURY: Well, there was no specific single moment. In fact, around the Tiananmen incident in 1989, I started to have doubts about the path we were on. But like many others in our government who were working on China, our, in retrospect, naive gullibility would continue. We would think, yes, this has been a human rights disaster, it's a setback for reform, but somehow it's really being carried out by older men in their nineties who will certainly pass away. The young reformers will take over and undo all this damage. That was my thinking into the '90s.

Looking back, President George H. W. Bush's decision to not fund the exiles who had left Beijing and gone to France—who had formed an exile government, elected a leader, and had a platform to bring democracy and free market to China—is a really painful memory for me. Because I was sent over to interview them in Paris and to see about the nature of the election.

But then we acted that way again in 1995 in the two aircraft carrier incidents, where another quite pro-China person like myself was the Secretary of Defense, Bill Perry. He was as shocked as I was that the Chinese would fire two long-range missiles over Taiwan, which, if something had gone wrong, would've killed many people down below. We sent two aircraft carriers to show our concern and that didn't really seem to calm down the situation.

You would think we'd all wake up and see we were dealing with a very different kind of China. But at that point we were told by the Chinese: "Well, it's your fault. You are encouraging this election in Taiwan for president, the first one. So, you've really started this." And there was some truth to that. We had encouraged an election in Taiwan. So once again, everybody, including me, began to fall back on, "Well, the reformers are in their nineties, you know, surely this is going to be a thing of the past." But each one of these passing incidents—I'm describing to you just two; there were actually six—would give me and others more concern, but we would always soothe ourselves by thinking "this is just a thing that will pass." We were so wrong.

RUDYARD GRIFFITHS: You've spent your life really studying China. Why do you think that this promise that we had all hoped for—that economic liberalization would lead to political liberalization—came to a crashing halt in the last ten years? Is it all about the specific leadership, or are there other dynamics in play in Chinese society that have allowed this to happen?

MICHAEL PILLSBURY: Well, it's both, because it's both the dynamics inside the leadership and that the influence of the hawks in China was concealed from outsiders. They were not like Steve Bannon going on television to give his views. The hawks were very powerful, but they were largely unknown to us, and they were Chinese generals and intelligence executives whom I had dealt with a lot. They concealed their views. So there was a certain amount of self-deception going on; we wanted so badly to believe everything was going to work out with China that their silence on their hawkish views let us deceive ourselves even further.

I can give you a vivid example. The Chinese military have translated my book into Chinese, and they've classified it. It's secret—only party members and military officers can buy it. So I asked a general whom I've seen again recently, "What's wrong?" and he said "Well, you're accusing us of deceiving America. But we never said we're going to have a multi-party democracy and a free market. We were just silent when *you* said that." And yes, that's true. If I go back over my notes, there's never a time when a Chinese hawk said to me, "Dr. Pillsbury, I swear we're going to have the New Hampshire primary system to elect our president some day." Never.

RUDYARD GRIFFITHS: I want to go back to your analysis that this Chinese stance of cloaking in deception goes back for millennia to the Warring States period. In other words, part of this is cultural, it's not just ideological.

MICHAEL PILLSBURY: Yes, but our misreading of this deception is also because of the way people like me are taught about China in graduate school. I got a Ph.D. from Columbia University focusing on Chinese politics. But I was not taught about the Warring States period. I was not taught about the importance of deception. I learned that from the Chinese themselves. They have their own internal textbooks about how to conduct foreign relations and how to do military strategy. I and others got hold of those books very late in the game and then we began to realize: "Oh my God. They're saying deception is the most important tool to use with a superior power, until the point where you can surpass it."

And the Chinese have this wonderful proverb that many people who read the book pick up on — "Don't ask the weight of the cauldrons." It comes from a story from the Warring States period, in which a country leader who wants to take over the empire accidently asks the grandson of the emperor, "How heavy are those cauldrons in the imperial palace?" Most Chinese proverbs are very vivid, and the sign of a civilized person is for you to know these proverbs.

So, don't ask the weight of the cauldrons. Some people say this is what Xi Jinping has done now. He's revealed his hand too soon. He's under criticism for provoking the trade fight with President Trump and for the South China Sea militarization that he promised Obama they wouldn't do. So he's become more arrogant than a Chinese leader should be and he's under criticism.

By the way, I found this in the 2011 Munk Debates book *Does the 21st Century Belong to China?*, in which Niall Ferguson is telling you that China has become arrogant and is behaving in ways that they'll come to regret.

RUDYARD GRIFFITHS: I'm sure you've confronted critics who would say: "Look, to ascribe to the Chinese some kind of cultural tendency toward deception is to rhetorically back our way into the Yellow Peril. To see these people somehow as other from us, incapable of seeing the world as we see it."

MICHAEL PILLSBURY: Absolutely, it's "How could I be so stupid or racist to think that only the Chinese practise deception." Actually those Chinese strategy textbooks I mentioned often compare Western deception techniques and give enormous praise to the amount of deception Westerners have used. One example is the Normandy landing. I actually had not known that we and the British and the Canadians bombed Calais a lot. Our pilots were killed, our planes were shot down, and it was all for a deception that the invasion would come through Calais, which is closer to Britain than Normandy is. So, the Chinese praised this. They say this is how World War II was won.

There's another famous deception where the British and Americans got a corpse and let it float out of a submarine ashore in Spain. The Nazis look at him and go, "Wow, he's got a briefcase handcuffed to his wrist." They open it up. The briefcase has got metro tickets, opera tickets, and a war plan of when the Americans are going to invade France in the south. It's totally false, totally concocted back in London by Eisenhower and Churchill. And it works. The Chinese love this. So, I don't think this focus on deception and how it works sometimes is racist. I don't think I'm "othering" the Chinese. The textbooks are very clear that deception only works if you're trusted. Your target has got to believe you're not a deceptive kind of person.

RUDYARD GRIFFITHS: Final question, and it's about a phrase that you know well: the Thucydides Trap. This is a reference to Thucydides, the historian of Ancient Greece, who posited that the rise of Athens so threatened Sparta that it made war inevitable. And if you look over the last five hundred years for analogues to the conflict between Sparta and Athens, you see roughly sixteen or so examples of these kind of rivalries, and roughly 75 percent of those examples led to war. Are we at real risk here of seeing the United States and China fall into the Thucydides Trap?

MICHAEL PILLSBURY: I would agree with the last chapter in Henry Kissinger's book *On China*. He is worried about a war on what he calls a World War I scale. That means the kind of war with millions dead on both sides. I think there's another possibility, which is an accidental war. We've got some Chinese hawks in the past few months saying, "The next time the Americans come through Chinese waters, we Chinese should send a ship to either sink them or attack them." Maybe this is just a couple of crazy hawks, but I happen to know them both and I think they have some influence inside the Chinese government. So an inadvertent, accidental war is one possibility.

As for a major World War I type of conflict happening, Kissinger is very clear. He explains that the way this could happen is if hawks in either Beijing or Washington take control of the government—I think he means through elections in the case of Washington—which will move us down the path toward war.

So no, I wouldn't say this is impossible. As recently as fifteen years ago, we had an informal taboo that no U.S. military journal—army, navy, air force, marine corps— could have articles about war with China. It was a forbidden topic partly because it's provocative, and partly because the chances were so low. Now, in the past three years, all of our journals have had many articles on how to win a war with China—new technology, new deployments, better intelligence.

On the Chinese side, officials used to conceal from me that they ever thought about a war with America; that was all Korean War and it had never happened again after. That stopped about five years ago. They now refer quite openly to the types of wars that could break out, including as a result of our supporting another power. If we'd backed India two years ago in the border dispute involving Bhutan, the Chinese claim they would have tried to punish us militarily. So when both militaries are talking openly about how to win a war with each other and both are running military exercises involving the other country, it's got to be seen as at least mildly dangerous.

I don't agree with the political scientist Graham Allison's concept of the Thucydides Trap. The Chinese do agree with him, which is bad for Graham. Because the concept says that we are irrationally afraid of China and that will lead to war. But most people who are concerned about China say that we've got to head off war. We've got to increase the chances of reform in China. The dream hasn't been given up by me or others. So there are two dangers with the so-called Thucydides Trap. One, war looks like it's inevitable; and, two, the American and Western side's position has been based on wrong emotions. Somehow, we're irrationally afraid of poor little China, and this is going to cause war. I can't agree with that concept.

RUDYARD GRIFFITHS: As a student of China, you would understand the extent to which they would bridle at the idea that we're going to instill our values in them.

I mean, this is a country that suffered the consequences of the Opium Wars. That seems the height of Western arrogance.

MICHAEL PILLSBURY: Yes. It's very shrewd of you to point that out. I think it's why Xi Jinping became the head of the Chinese Communist Party in 2012 and president of China in 2013. He was not selected by previous leaders, as had been their system before. Xi Jinping had to defeat a relatively hawkish candidate named Bo Xilai, who's now in jail for life. He did that, I believe, by making an appeal to the hawks. His platform contained the exact sentiment you just expressed: that we can't stand for this, that we've got to come out more in the open, that China has to stand up; that we can't have these Westerners imposing their values, which is rock 'n' roll—he characterizes Western values in a way you might find inaccurate.

So, he was chosen and now he's surrounded himself with hawks. And we were lucky that the main negotiator in Washington for the first ten rounds of the current talks is a reformer, an economist who's written reform articles. But that's very rare these days, as most reformers have been put in prison.

KISHORE MAHBUBANI IN CONVERSATION WITH RUDYARD GRIFFITHS

RUDYARD GRIFFITHS: Kishore Mahbubani, thank you for coming to Toronto to be part of this debate. It's a real honour to have you here.

KISHORE MAHBUBANI: My pleasure.

RUDYARD GRIFFITHS: Let's jump right in and get your thoughts as to why, at this particular moment, tensions between China and the United States have reached this almost frenetic level over trade. What's going on?

KISHORE MAHBUBANI: Well, it's one of those events that could have been completely predicted in advance. It was inevitable. It was going to happen at some point in time because throughout history, the geopolitics of the time is driven by the relationship between the world's number-one power, which today is the United States, and the world's number-one emerging power, which today is China. And it's always at the point when the world's number-one emerging power is about to become bigger than the world's number-one power that tensions escalate.

So, it was going to happen at some point or another, and you can never tell exactly how it's going to happen, when it's going to happen — which is why I'm actually writing a book on U.S.-China relations this year. But what caused it to happen this year was, in part, the presidency of Donald Trump, who's got rather strange views on trade — he would not pass an Economics 101 exam on trade — and yet, despite this, everybody supports him. The only issue in America where Donald Trump gets broad bipartisan support is the stand he's taking against China on trade.

And clearly the Chinese have made some strategic mistakes in the way that they've handled the United States and American businessmen, and so to some extent they're paying a price for this too. But at the end of the day, the real issue is not trade; the real issue is something deeper. So even if the trade issue is solved today, tomorrow, or whenever, the dispute between the U.S. and China will escalate in the coming decades.

RUDYARD GRIFFITHS: We're going to talk about the liberal international order tonight, which is a somewhat loaded phrase, especially because of the word "liberal" that's stuck in there. How do you interpret the liberal international order? What are its liberal characteristics?

KISHORE MAHBUBANI: Well, you know, I have two advantages in terms of understanding the liberal international order. First, I've served as Singapore's ambassador to the U.N. for over ten years, so I have first-hand experience with how the heart of the liberal international order, which is the United Nations, works.

But the more important, second advantage is that I was born into an illiberal international order. It was in 1948 that I was born in Singapore. Singapore was a British colony and, basically, I wasn't even born a citizen; I was born a British "subject," but more truthfully a British "object."

So there's a contrast with what preceded 1945, when you had in a sense a few dominant states, the colonial states, running most of the world, making decisions for most of the world in a completely arbitrary fashion with no rules whatsoever. Which is why 1945, especially with the signing of the U.N. Charter, marks a watershed moment in world history, because suddenly it is decided that from now on people can determine their own futures. The Charter delegitimized colonialism, it delegitimized foreign intervention, and it created the notion of sovereignty. And I think that's one pillar of what the liberal international order is: you decide your own future.

The second pillar of the liberal international order is what I call the rules. And progressively, through the U.N., through other multilateral institutions, we have accumulated lots of rules on what countries can and cannot do. And the surprising thing about our world is that, most of the time, most countries obey these rules. And that's why, for example, if you look back before 1945, wars between states were very common. In an instant, countries would go to war. But progressively, interstate wars have become a sunset industry, and the chance of a human being dying in an interstate war today is the lowest it's ever been.

So these are the two big advances that have been made by the liberal international order: it's allowed the people to determine their own futures, and it's created a set of rules that all countries follow. And therefore, it's a liberal order.

RUDYARD GRIFFITHS: I thought you quite provocatively and rightly, in an essay for *Harper's Magazine*, flagged the fact that, when it comes to understanding the impacts of two different models of economic leadership—China's versus the United States'—China might have a pretty good story to tell in terms of their record of economic accomplishment in contrast to the picture in the United States of stagnant wages, stagnant incomes, and growing economic inequality. Do you see part of this debate going on right now as a debate between two different economic orders? Or is there a consensus as to what the global economic order should be?

KISHORE MAHBUBANI: I think there's nothing wrong with the American economic system, but something has gone fundamentally wrong in the American political system, because the political system acted as a kind of adjudicator to ensure that, as economic growth happened, you would distribute the fruits more or less equitably.

But one of the most shocking things about the United

26

States is that, for reasons that we still don't understand fully, it's the only major developed country where the average income of the bottom 50 percent—let me repeat that: five-zero percent—has gone down over a thirty-year period. So, something has gone wrong in the balance of the society and how you allocate the fruits of economic growth.

Another shocking statistic I have in my book *Has the West Lost It?* is that two-thirds of American family households don't have $500 in emergency cash. So that's another thing that's gone wrong. It's not the economic system; the economy is growing. But how do you distribute the fruits? This is where fundamental issues of taxation come in.

And one of the points I'm going to make about the U.S.-China conflict is that what's happened is that the major American political institutions have in a sense been seized or taken over by big money, which influences the institutions' decisions. So, the capacity of government to act as an impartial referee and umpire to redistribute the fruits of economic growth has gone. And as a result, vast numbers of Americans are now suffering. And that also explains the anger that led to the election of Donald Trump.

RUDYARD GRIFFITHS: Stepping back and thinking about some of the arguments that your opponents will put forward tonight, one of them obviously will be that China has given up on economic liberalization, that it is fundamentally an authoritarian regime that is a threat to democracy and to a capital-*l* Liberal vision of the liberal international order. Do you feel that's a fair criticism of what's happened in China?

KISHORE MAHBUBANI: I would say one has to make a fundamental distinction between the liberal *international* order and the liberal *domestic* order. And China clearly does not belong to the category of liberal domestic order. But there's no fundamental contradiction with a country that is non-democratic, like China, behaving according to the rules of the liberal international order.

A lot of confusion is created fundamentally by the word "liberal." I'm going to quote just two scholars in the international relations field. I just asked John Mearsheimer, the leading realist thinker in America, "John, can I quote you as saying that America is a bigger threat to the liberal international order than China?" He said, "Kishore, go ahead." So, I have his permission.

And then look at the recent statement that John Ikenberry made. Ikenberry is probably the leading writer on liberal international order issues. And he said, "I never thought I would see the day when the liberal international order would be killed—not by murder but by suicide." It is the proponents of the liberal international order, the United States, who are the primary killers of the order because the United States is walking away from its constraining rules.

So, the paradox we have in the world today is that China is not a democracy and America is, but it's a democracy that is a bigger threat to the liberal international order than a non-democracy.

RUDYARD GRIFFITHS: Just to push that line of questioning a little bit further, it is interesting to see the extent to which, at least in the Western media, we are fed a steady diet of news about China's authoritarian sins of omission and commission — whether it's the internment of large numbers of their Uyghur population, or the seeming adoption of a mass system of state surveillance. Are we interpreting the world through the thought categories of the past? Have we gone back to a kind of Cold War mythology — or maybe even pre–Cold War, maybe a World War II mythology — that this is somehow not just a struggle about trade but a struggle for democracy against an evil, as some people would characterize it, authoritarian regime?

KISHORE MAHBUBANI: Here's the strange thing about Western media and thinkers becoming progressively more and more negative about China's track record in the past few decades: If you ask the Chinese people what, in their opinion, have been the best thirty years for their country in the past 3,000 years, since Chinese history began, they will say the last thirty years. Because you've seen this dramatic removal of poverty, 800 million people rescued from absolute poverty.

When I first went to China in 1980, people couldn't choose where to live, where to work, what to wear, where to study. And certainly, no Chinese citizen could travel overseas. That was close to forty years ago. Now if you go to China, you see that people can choose where to live, where to work, what to wear, where to study. And amazingly enough for a Communist gulag state — a country like the Soviet Union, which allowed zero tourists — each year 134 million Chinese leave freely and travel overseas.

RUDYARD GRIFFITHS: And guess what? They come back.

KISHORE MAHBUBANI: An amazing 134 million Chinese — who could choose to stay overseas — return to China freely. If you believe that voting with your feet is a very powerful voting mechanism, these people are saying, "I love this country. It's been good for me." And why is that so?

And so I think the fundamental problem in Western perceptions of China is that their minds have become trapped in an artificial time bubble of two hundred years of Western domination of world history, which is coming to an end, and therefore they are unable to enter into other thought bubbles that exist within very different worldviews.

From the Chinese point of view, one clear lesson from 2,200 years of continuous Chinese history is that when the centre is weak, the people suffer; when the centre is strong, people benefit. So strong leaders like Xi Jinping are popular in China. People like him. Their lives are better.

So how is it that a country like the United States of America, which has a population of 300 million-plus — one-quarter of the Chinese population — and a political history that is only one-tenth as long, how is it that this nouveau riche who just arrived on the political scene is saying, "I know what's best for you, China. And even though you've had 2,000 years of history, you don't know what's good for yourselves"?

And I think that at some point in time, if you're a Chinese leader you have to understand and live within your own political culture. And there are tremendous constraints in running China—because each day that China stays together, with 1.4 billion people working together, is a miracle. It's incredibly hard work. It requires a kind of governance which is not, by the way, completely top-down; it requires an understanding of what the people can accept, will not accept, and so on and so forth.

Because if 1.4 billion people decide to rise up, no government can stop them. And so this is the Chinese political dynamic that is operating. And those of us who live outside should not presume that we know better than the Chinese what is good for them.

RUDYARD GRIFFITHS: Final question: you come from Singapore; you've represented Singapore as a diplomat; you lived there. This debate is originating out of Canada. What should smaller countries, like Canada and Singapore, do to thrive—let's hope—but maybe simply survive the clash of these two big global powers? Where is our advantage, if any, in this scenario? Or, frankly, is this going to be just an exceedingly difficult period geopolitically for middle powers?

KISHORE MAHBUBANI: I think the first thing we should remember is the wisdom contained in an old Sri Lankan proverb, which says: "When elephants fight, the grass suffers. When elephants make love, the grass also suffers." So, whether or not the global powers fight or make love, we're going to get into trouble.

It's important for us, number one, to figure out what kind of environment is the best for constraining these great powers. And fortunately for us, this is where the liberal international order is so important. The United Nations has created all kinds of rules that in a sense act like constraining nets on these superpowers.

One thing that Canada and Singapore should do together, in a common interest we have, is to strengthen the United Nations as much as possible. I remember when I was ambassador to the U.N., and trying to strengthen its rules and treaties and so forth, I found that Canada was one of the strongest partners we could work with because Canada also deeply believed in multilateralism — although you went through a phase where, to my surprise, you actually walked away from multilateralism, and I was very puzzled because that doesn't serve Canada's national interests. But I'm glad you're coming back to the position that you used to hold.

So I think the one thing we need to do is to realize that the post-1945 rule space, the liberal international order, is a huge gift and asset for small and medium-sized states, and we should work together to strengthen it as much as possible, knowing full well that the big powers in their own way will try to reduce it — especially, unfortunately, the United States. And in fact the conclusion of my book *Has the West Lost It?* is that the best way for the United States to constrain the future China is to use U.N. rules. They will be a more effective net than anything else.

HUIYAO WANG IN CONVERSATION
WITH RUDYARD GRIFFITHS

RUDYARD GRIFFITHS: Huiyao Wang, thank you so much for coming to Toronto. It's great to have you here as part of this debate.

I want to get your views on why you think China-U.S. relations at this moment are in a period of tension. What has been the catalyst for that? What's brought this whole situation about?

HUIYAO WANG: Thank you for having me. I think we have seen that for the decades China has been open, it has been gradually increasing its economic influence. It's now become the second-largest economy, and so many U.S. companies are working in China. So the interests of both countries are so much more intertwined than ever before. But, as the mutual interests deepen, there's bound to be some disagreements, problems, and frictions.

But I think that the current situation is led by President Trump, who took office and pursued an America-first approach, and *that* actually started this trade tension. Since 2001, China has joined the World Trade Organization, and its GDP has gone up almost ten times. It is probably going to be the largest economy in the world in ten to fifteen years' time. So, I think there is also an issue adjusting on both sides.

Also, China has readily participated in, fallen in love with, and strongly defended the multilateral system, while the U.S. is pulling out of a lot of agreements. His first day in office, President Trump pulled out of the Trans-Pacific Partnership, and then the Paris Climate Change Agreement and quite a few United Nations organizations — such as UNESCO — and he has threatened to pull out of the WTO as well. So, I think there's a lot of points-scoring now.

But I think that another big reason for the tensions is that the U.S. looked at the normally low trade deficit and said, "Oh, there's a $375 billion trade deficit." But they may not have realized that half of that was exports by American or foreign companies. So, China has the appearance of that but may not necessarily have the benefit. Also, the service trade is not counted in that number. China has three million tourists visiting the United States, spending $30 billion, which is not counted. China has half a million students in the United States, contributing another $20 billion; that's also not counted.

It's also the effect of a lack of communication.

RUDYARD GRIFFITHS: Let's talk about that. Is there frustration in China about the extent to which China's demonstrable commitment to a lot of multilateral institutions is underestimated? The Paris Accord, the Law of the Sea: you can go on and on and look at these different multilateral bodies that the United States has either withdrawn from or criticized. But it often seems that China, at least in the West, gets painted as being as unilateral as the United States. Why is that happening? And how do people in China interpret this?

HUIYAO WANG: I think there's quite a bit of a culture difference involved. I think China, first of all, pursued a different development model than the Western countries. I think there was some early expectation that China would converge with the Western model, but that obviously has not been the case. As Deng Xiaoping said, it doesn't matter if it's a white cat or a black cat, as long as it catches mice. So, if its own model works for China, well, China maybe should stick to that.

And then China in the last four decades has been able to lift 800 million people out of poverty. China has contributed to the world and is now the second-largest donor to the United Nations. Also, China has set up the Asian Infrastructure Investment Bank [AIIB] with ninety-five member countries, including a lot of Western countries, though not the U.S. or Japan. So China is doing a lot of multilateral efforts, particularly its Belt and Road Initiative. China has actually spent $40 or $50 billion already on that in a number of countries.

RUDYARD GRIFFITHS: I want to ask you about Belt and Road, because it's an interesting facet of this debate in terms of how an issue can be viewed in two very different ways. There's an argument that the Belt and Road Initiative is an example of multilateralism, that 126 countries have signed co-operation agreements, that China is spending hundreds of billions of dollars to build this infrastructure, that it's increased trade, it's lowered shipping times.

Yet there's a perception in the West at times that this is a hostile move, that China is practising this "debt-trap diplomacy" to ensnare these countries in a vassal-like relationship. Again, how can two such opposite things be true at the same time?

HUIYAO WANG: First of all, Belt and Road only started about five or six years ago. So it will take time for Western countries to gradually realize its benefits. But since the 2008 financial crisis—probably even since the Marshall Plan to build up Western Europe after World War II— there's been no major stimulus from the world to help the economic growth of developing countries.

China has benefited from other countries in the past. All countries come to China. So, for the last four decades China has cultivated and developed this capacity for infrastructure, which is now probably the most advanced in the world, with high-speed trains and one billion smartphone users, and is now becoming a cashless society. So that kind of newly developed expertise could be shared with the vast number of developing countries. Just like a venture capitalist, China is putting up the seed money.

And let's have an A round, a B round, a C round. Let's all get together.

So the principles of Belt and Road are that it should be jointly consulted, jointly built, and jointly shared. It is actually designed around a multilateral approach, but I think it probably still needs more help. I'm glad to see that the second Belt and Road conference in Beijing just last month had forty heads of state attend and 150 countries represented.

But I think there's a point there; we could make it more multilateral. For example, we can more involve the World Bank, the Asian Development Bank, the African Development Bank, and all the other banks. We can also get the Organisation for Economic Co-operation and Development and the Paris Club involved. I think, first of all, we should not take a position on that at the very beginning, because then why would so many developing countries participate?

We've been lacking that kind of a stimulus package since the financial crisis. So, it's probably a shot in the arm of the global economy that China makes these injections of capital and of infrastructure expertise that could link the world. According to the World Bank, Belt and Road could increase the GDP of the world by 0.1 percent and probably cut down by 1 to 2 percent the cost of trade among the countries.

So, Belt and Road is a very good initiative. It's not perfect, of course; it still needs a lot of improvement. It's just started. That's precisely why we need more countries to participate. I'm glad to see Italy as the first G7 country participating, and Switzerland, Luxembourg, and Greece have just come in. I think that if more developing countries, and the United States, join hands with China, Belt and Road could be the impetus for the next generation of global stimulus, to carry the world into a much better, more prosperous future.

If we fight on that, if nobody can initiate the plan unless the U.S. does, then the world will lack an engine. China is already part of a global engine.

RUDYARD GRIFFITHS: Do you think that that is really the core of this debate? That the United States is feeling increasingly uncomfortable and anxious about losing its economic and military global supremacy? Something it has enjoyed now, unbroken, since the fall of the Berlin Wall in 1989.

HUIYAO WANG: It could be. I was at Harvard many years ago, at the Kennedy School, and the professor and founding dean Graham Allison proposed a very interesting theory of the Thucydides Trap. He just spoke at my think tank about a month and a half ago. He said that there could be competition between a rising power and an existing power, but that there are many ways of peaceful coexistence. It doesn't have to be a strategic rivalry. If the U.S. perceives China as a strategic rival, that sends the wrong signal. They should be co-operative; probably a co-operative rivalry. But I think in the end that if the world economy is benefiting from Belt and Road, then China should really get more involved with the

Western countries and think about how to improve the initiative. Make it work. Like the Asian Infrastructure Investment Bank, Belt and Road has ninety-five member countries. India is the largest recipient, and Canada, the U.K., Germany, and France all are member countries. So if AIIB can have this involvement, why not the Belt and Road Initiative?

Also, there's a lot of talk about debt traps, but we just had a new study by the Rogan Group, basically saying there aren't many concrete examples. So there are a lot of theories that I can see, you know, about intellectual property theft, technology transfers, debt traps. But please give me a concrete example, because we haven't seen many of them.

RUDYARD GRIFFITHS: Are you surprised at the extent to which it seems that in many of the current negotiations going on between the United States and China there's an assumption on the part of the United States that China needs to adopt its model? In other words, whatever reforms of processes that the United States has, China has to have these as well before you can have "a deal." How is that interpreted in China? Because it seems like an extension of a very troubling history between Asia and the rest of the world, where in the past, whenever the West could, it would not only impose its values on Asia but also force China into a position of subservience. Are we repeating bad habits of the past?

HUIYAO WANG: It actually worries me. I don't exclude that maybe there could be people thinking in racial ways. For example, recently, a U.S. State Department official, Kiron Skinner, said there could be a clash of civilizations, and it's the first clash of Caucasians versus Asians. That sounds very racial, certainly coming from an official of the U.S. government. So, I'm very, very taken aback by that.

I think we should probably avoid this Cold War mentality. We are living in a much-developed world now; not seventy or eighty years ago when every country was isolated, everybody was self-sufficient, and everybody was misinformed or couldn't access information. Now everybody is well informed. The world is so intertwined, and we are so dependent on each other. Seventy or eighty years ago, there was no value chain. Now there's a full-fledged value chain. We can't live without each other. Like it or not, we have to live together.

I think this is why we haven't seen any major war in the last seven decades. Trade — goods movement, capital movement — has supported this prosperous world. We want to keep that with our new initiative; we want to have a new drive and new impetus. Now, after getting help from all the other countries for the past four decades, help from Western countries and the liberal order system, it's time for China to contribute. China doesn't want to take the U.S.'s position or be the policeman of the world. China's military budget is only a quarter of the U.S.'s. The next eight countries' military spending combined is not even equal to the U.S.'s, so we shouldn't worry that much.

RUDYARD GRIFFITHS: Final question: Do you see this current state of tension between China and the United States as something that's transitory, that has to deal with the personalities that are here right now, or are you concerned that we're creating distrust and real damage to the relationship that could have repercussions well into the future?

HUIYAO WANG: I think it will be very devastating if U.S.-China trade relations are not properly handled and solved. You see that in today's market the U.S. is tumbling and China, of course, suffers greatly. The business communities of both countries, in particular, cannot afford poor relations. General Motors and Ford sell more cars in China than in the United States. China is Apple's second-largest market, and Walmart purchases 20 percent of goods from China to supply U.S. supermarkets. So it's really not in the interest of either government to fight this trade war.

I think the multinationals have a lot of legitimate concerns, but China just passed the foreign investment law in March, forbidding any technology transfer. Any Intellectual Property Rights violations will be severely punished. No government should be allowed to do any of these kinds of activities. Foreign companies should be treated the same as Chinese companies. So, you see, China has already taken a lot of actions to correct that misconception. There may have been some incident that has caused that experience. But, I think in general, China is very sincere about fixing this.

Even with President Trump, with this threat, China

is still open. Because you have to be responsible as the second-largest economy. You've got to think about the world. It's not just a matter between China and the U.S. It's actually going to affect the whole world. If the two biggest economies don't get along, all the other countries suffer. Then all the blue-collar workers and all the people around the world suffer.

So I think it's really the responsibility of the U.S. and China to get along on those issues. And if trade goes on, the prosperity continues, and world economy growth continues, then we can really fight the setbacks of globalization. We can really fight all those issues, such as climate change and terrorism. I think there will be severe consequences if we don't handle this issue properly.

China and the West

Be it resolved: China is a threat to the
liberal international order.

Pro: H. R. McMaster and Michael Pillsbury
Con: Kishore Mahbubani and Huiyao Wang

May 9, 2019
Toronto, Ontario

RUDYARD GRIFFITHS: Ladies and gentlemen, welcome. Great to have you here tonight. Thank you. For the Munk Debate on China, my name is Rudyard Griffiths and it's my privilege to have the opportunity to organize this debate series and to once again serve as your moderator.

I want to start tonight by welcoming the North America–wide audience tuning in to this debate on television via our partner CPAC — Canada's Public Affairs Channel — C-SPAN across the continental United States, and on WNED and its PBS sister stations. It's great to have that audience with us this evening. A warm hello also to our friends watching right now via the website of our exclusive social media partner, Facebook.com. And finally, hello to you, the over 3,000 people who've filled Roy Thomson Hall to capacity for yet another Munk Debate.

A special thanks to our premium members and our

subscribers for your generous support for more and better debate on the big issues of the day. We cannot do this series without you. Our ability, year in and year out, to bring some of the world's biggest minds and best thinkers to this stage would not be possible without the commitment and the generosity of one foundation and one family. So please join me in a round of applause for the Peter and Melanie Munk Foundation and the Munk family. Thank you all for your generous support of this series. Peter's philanthropic legacy lives on.

This evening, we'll focus on the geopolitical issue of the moment. It's been on our screens all day today. It's been dominating the news all week. It's the issue of the impact of a resurgent China on the international balance of power. We're going to explore this critical issue by asking the question: Is China a threat to the liberal international order?

Now, I think it's important for us to just spend a moment here to define some of our terms. What do we mean by this phrase, the "liberal international order"? I see it as a catchphrase for the world that many of us have grown up in, a world that has favoured the free movement of people, ideas, goods, and capital. It's a world order guaranteed by the rule of law: setting rules, observing rules. It's been supported by a broad commitment over decades to pursuing multilateralism over unilateralism as a way of decision-making. It's a world that's given nation states the capacity and the ability for self-determination, and it's also a world that has been guaranteed to a large extent over five decades now by the military power and economic strength of the United States of America.

So we're going to ask some tough questions this evening. We're going to ask: Are China's political interests — Beijing's vision of the world and how it should be — incompatible with the values and institutions of the liberal international order, or is this view just a fundamental misunderstanding of how China sees the world? Instead of being its enemy, is Beijing, in fact, an important ally to the liberal international order in an era of multipolar competition and confusion, and an era of seemingly rising American unilateralism?

Let's find out by getting our debaters out here centre stage and our debate underway. Arguing for tonight's resolution, "Be it resolved: China is a threat to the liberal international order," is America's former national security advisor and a celebrated military commander. Ladies and gentlemen, please welcome General H. R. McMaster.

General McMaster's debating partner tonight is one of America's most influential advisors on China today. He's counselled multiple U.S. administrations and played a key role in informing President Donald Trump's China strategy. Please welcome, from Washington, D.C., Michael Pillsbury.

Now, one great team of debaters deserves another, and speaking against tonight's motion is the Singaporean diplomat, bestselling author, and former president of the United Nations Security Council Kishore Mahbubani.

Kishore's debating partner is someone who's made the trip to be here this evening from Beijing. He's one of China's leading thinkers on globalization and the founder and leader of the influential Beijing-based Center for China and Globalization. Please welcome Huiyao Wang.

It's time for our first live audience vote here in the hall on tonight's resolution. Can I see the results, please? Seventy-six percent of you believe that China is a threat to the liberal international order. Only 24 percent opposed. So, an interesting start to the evening, but remember, we're now going to see how fluid your minds are.

We're now going to vote on a second question: Are you open to changing your mind tonight? Depending on what you hear on the stage between our various debaters, could you change your mind? Could your opinion be swayed from one side of the hall to the other?

Are you open to changing your vote? Apparently, 83 percent of you are. So this is a very fluid debate, gentlemen. Either side could move public opinion to their case for the resolution.

Let's get our debate underway and go to our opening statements. We're going to put six minutes on the clock for each debater. We've agreed on the order in advance. H. R. McMaster, please kick us off.

H. R. MCMASTER: Thanks, Rudyard. Good evening. It is a privilege to be here in this wonderful forum.

Under President Xi Jinping, the Chinese Communist Party has resolved to strengthen its grip on power, take centre stage in the world, and make good on Xi's pledge to lead the development of new rules and a new international order sympathetic to Chinese interests. The Chinese Communist Party is not only strengthening an internal system that stifles human freedom and extends its authoritarian control, but it is also exporting that model across the world and undermining the liberal international order.

I ask that at the conclusion of tonight's debate you answer tonight's question — "Is China a threat to the liberal international order?" — in the affirmative. The Chinese Communist Party poses a threat not only to the Chinese people but also to the rest of the world.

First, let's consider the liberal international order and why we might want to preserve it. The liberal order is not exclusively North American, European, or Western. Its key components are representative government, the rule of law, freedom of speech and freedom of the press, the right to privacy and freedom of religion, and free market economies that allow those who are entrepreneurial, work hard, and contribute to society to build better lives for themselves and their families and their communities.

I believe that Canadians care about our liberal order. As a model democracy and a founding member of that order in the wake of two disastrous world wars, Canadians know that liberalism is not only an ideology but also a system that protects their rights in Canada's mosaic society. The free world's approach to China for the past three decades was predicated on the assumption that China would *not* threaten our liberal international order. China, we believed, would inevitably converge with the West, liberalize its economy, and, ultimately, liberalize its political system. To accelerate that transformation, we welcomed China into our order, opened our markets, invested our capital, trained Chinese engineers, scientists, and even officers of the People's Liberation Army. But as happens sometimes in life, we were disappointed.

We underestimated the strength of the party in resisting reform, and we underestimated the role that ideology plays in driving the policies of the party. Xi has reinvigorated ideology to an extent not seen since Mao's Cultural Revolution, which killed tens of millions of Chinese. Chairman Xi is purging the party to strengthen his control. He punished 1.5 million officials — over three times the total number of the federal public service of Canada. Xi implemented mandatory study sessions and even apps on Xi Jinping thought. The party is harnessing new technologies to shut out alternative sources of information while creating a surveillance police state more intrusive than Big Brother's in George Orwell's novel *Nineteen Eighty-Four.*

Ethnic and religious minorities are subject to the worst forms of oppression. In Jinjiang, 1.5 to as many as 3 million people are in concentration camps undergoing a campaign of brainwashing designed to erase their religious and cultural identity. Construction of new camps is underway. The party raids universities; student activists disappear, only to reappear months later on confession videos. Hundreds of lawyers, legal assistants, and professors have been detained. Books on the rule of law are removed from university shelves and destroyed. Censorship of all media and communications is the party's obsession. There are no alternative perspectives to counter the party's steady diet of propaganda, much of it anti-Western and anti-Canadian and anti–liberal international order. The party combined anti-West and anti-Canadian propaganda with hostage-taking after the legal detainment of a Chinese company executive for charges of bank fraud in the United States.

China has expanded its propaganda efforts overseas. Those efforts, recently exposed in studies in Australia, New Zealand, and the United States, shape popular opinion in ways that support China's goals. Chinese students overseas are under surveillance and unable to engage in the free exchange of ideas essential to higher education. The United Front even creates fake organizations that then fake the prime minister's signature on fake documents. The party wants to mute criticism of its most egregious aggression, such as its attempt to own the South China Sea.

For our companies to do business in China, the party demands that they and their employees support China's foreign policy on Tibet, Taiwan, and other issues, to obscure facts such as how China, while feigning commitment to reducing greenhouse emissions, is poisoning the global environment and using its Belt and Road Initiative—

RUDYARD GRIFFITHS: Okay. We're going to let you pick up some of those points in your rebuttal, which you're going to get after all the opening statements. So Huiyao Wang, you're up next with your opening remarks. Thank you.

HUIYAO WANG: Thank you, Rudyard, and good evening, ladies and gentlemen and distinguished panellists here. It's really a great honour to be in Toronto. General McMaster has just painted a very dark picture of China, but I think maybe we have to look at it more objectively.

I'd like to tell you a personal story. You know, I'm a person who lived through the Cultural Revolution. Some forty years ago, I was working in the countryside and making five cents a day. But thirty-five years ago, I came to Canada. The first city I came to was Toronto, and I studied at the University of Toronto. It's a great university. And you know, the first day I went into class somebody came up to me and said, "Can I touch you?" I said, "Why not?" Then he touched me. He said, "Oh, I touched someone from Red China!" Oh, from Red China, so scary! So, I hope that kind of scary won't come back. To tell you the reason why, I have three proposals to make.

The first: since China opened up, it has been a great beneficiary of the liberal international order. The U.S. set up this wonderful liberal international order, including the United Nations, World Bank, IMF [International Monetary Fund], WTO, you name it. China embraced them all, so that in the last four decades China has lifted 800 million people out of poverty. Actually, that accounts for more than 10 percent of the global population and also corresponds to 70 percent of the global poverty reduction.

Larry Summers, the former president of Harvard, came to our think tank about two months ago and said that the transformation in China probably will go down in history as a process larger than the Industrial Revolution. Since China joined the WTO, China's GDP has gone up ten times, because China embraced the liberal international order. China is the largest trading nation; over a hundred countries benefit from Chinese economic activity. China also contributes over 35 percent of the GDP of the world. So it's become an engine of the world economy.

China has become now the second-largest economy in the world. Every year 150 million tourists from China travel around the world, spending $200 billion for local economies. Since it has opened up, China has sent over six million students all over the world, including to Canada, such a great country.

Second: China is a great contributor to the liberal international order. And do you know what? China is actually the second-largest donor to the United Nations. It's also the second-largest peacekeeping-sending country among the permanent Security Council members. And China has actually committed to the Paris Agreement. The U.S. has backed off, but China didn't avoid its responsibility and duties.

Moreover, China has set up the Asian Infrastructure Investment Bank. And this has been embraced globally. Canada is a member, the U.K. is a member, France is a member, Germany is a member. There are ninety-five members and, do you know who is the largest recipient of the AIIB? India.

President Xi launched the Belt and Road Initiative five years ago, but it is still in the process of becoming more and more beneficial. Since the initiative started, it has invested $44 billion U.S. into the Belt and Road countries. China has now signed 127 memoranda of understanding with countries — including Italy, including Switzerland, including Luxembourg—and with thirty international lending institutions.

So, China is really contributing, because China has benefited for the last four decades from the help of the world. It's time for China to contribute. Belt and Road is an initiative to do that. It's not perfect. It still needs improvement, but the World Bank just released a report that if Belt and Road is conducted, world trading costs will be cut down by 1 to 2 percent. The global economy will grow by 0.1 percent.

Number three: China is a great opportunity for the global liberal system. Today, J. P. Morgan just concluded its fifteenth China global conference in Beijing. Nicolas Aguzin, the chairman of J. P. Morgan Asia-Pacific, said that the growth of the Chinese economy has benefited all countries in the world. China is now also an opportunity. China has established 850,000 companies. The U.S. has started up 68,000 companies in China. It is the largest market of the world now, with 400 million members of the middle class; in the next one hundred years there will be 800 million. Today's *Globe and Mail* said Canada's exports to China for the last twelve years increased by 12 percent, and last year by 18 percent. So, it's a great market for Canada. Thank you.

RUDYARD GRIFFITHS: Thank you. And again, we'll get more time in the rebuttals to finish off your points. So, Michael Pillsbury, you're up next with your opening statement.

MICHAEL PILLSBURY: Thank you. Well, it's possible to agree

with everything Henry Wang just said — all these good things about China — but still vote for our position on the resolution, that China currently — and I'm going to give you the year I think the problem began — that China currently is a threat to the global international order.

I think the problem began about 2011, Rudyard, just about the time when you had Henry Kissinger here for the first Munk Debate on China. About that time there was a power struggle in China over who should become the leader. And there was a movement called "singing red songs" that we didn't pay much attention to at the time. Dr. Kissinger actually went to Sichuan to hear this contender for leader, Bo Xilai, singing the "red songs." At the time, someone paid careful attention — Xi Jinping. He also made a visit there. He began to adopt the language of the hardliners in China. He won the race.

Chinese politics is not like the New Hampshire primary or debates on television where you can say, you know, things like, "You're sleepy," or "No, you're low energy!" Chinese politics is played like a blood sport. The gentleman who lost actually went to jail. Bo Xilai and all of his supporters went to jail. The issue at the time was whether to continue the liberal reforms that China had begun as early as 1980: joining the World Bank and the IMF; studying the U.N. specialized agencies, joining every single one of them, and taking over leadership in a number of them. All that began to go down in the battles of the '90s. We all thought, "No, the reformers are going to recover," but they didn't. The hardliners were back.

So, this back and forth now looks like something really

serious has happened in China. Large numbers of reformers are in jail. It's a bit unfair to ask Henry to represent China tonight because his think tank is one of the top hundred most influential in the world. But when I visit his think tank, do I see the hardliners come out? No. They're winning. They're in power. I see the reformers and the good economists and the good part of China in Henry's think tank. But they're losing.

Let's look forward to 2049, which some Chinese say is the end date of the Hundred-Year Marathon, a phrase I borrowed for the title of my book. They say that this marathon, which will be peaceful, will be over in 2049 with China's GDP three times America's. The beginning of the conduct we've been seeing over the last few years — which began under President Obama — is China breaking commitments and breaking promises by saying, for example, "We will never militarize the South China Sea" — which was a voluntary promise by President Xi. As they say, the ink was barely dry when we began to see missiles and military deployments in the South China Sea.

So there's now a long list of rights that seem to be gone, which H. R. has given you — freedom of religion, freedom of speech, freedom of assembly, free market — they've capped the free market so that it appears that even the percent that's free in China is being reduced — freedom from Communist Party control of your company. So, the question becomes, how to turn China around? Can we get back to a co-operative China, with the reformers in power and the hardliners — I hate to say it — the hardliners in jail. How to do that?

One way is to vote for our side of the resolution. And then you will head off what Graham Allison of Harvard has called the almost inevitable war that's coming.

It's not just the United States, by the way. You had a great statesman in Lester Pearson. He was Canada's ambassador to the United States in 1945. He participated in the creation of the U.N. Charter. He was proposed to be the first U.N. secretary-general, but was vetoed by the Soviets. He was proposed again in 1953, but vetoed again by the Soviets. So, Canada's always been involved deeply and has a stake in this liberal international order.

I have to say, in conclusion, that if you look ahead to 2049, everything seems to get worse. Pollution gets worse. The number of what China calls its cancer villages increases. Censorship increases. We've now had 150 Tibetan monks light themselves on fire in suicidal protest. That gets worse. The one to three million Muslims in concentration camps gets worse. Perhaps all the reformers will be in jail. Perhaps we won't be able to have Henry Wang come back in 2049 because he'll be in jail!

It's a pretty grim picture, and me, I'm nostalgic for the '80s. When I was working for President Reagan, we sold six weapon systems to China. We sold torpedoes. So that's the vision of Chinese-American co-operation, but it's not what we're seeing happen now. So I'm hoping, Rudyard, that the Munk Debate results will help us in getting China back to where it should be.

I think I should finish by saying the Chinese have done an excellent job of understanding the United Nations system. Kishore was Singapore's ambassador twice —

RUDYARD GRIFFITHS: Tripped up by the clock, Michael. You're going to have to add that to your rebuttal.

MICHAEL PILLSBURY: I'm hoping to hear from him about China and the U.N.

RUDYARD GRIFFITHS: We've saved our last opening statement for Kishore Mahbubani. We're going to put six minutes on the clock for you right now, Kishore.

KISHORE MAHBUBANI: Thank you. You know, I'm very happy to be back in Canada because I consider myself an honorary Canadian. I studied at Dalhousie, got a master's. I even got an honorary doctorate, spent five summers in Chester, and for ten years I was non-resident high commissioner to Canada. And I learned something very good from a very well-known Canadian, Wayne Gretzky. He said, "Skate to where the puck is going, not to where it is." And H. R. McMaster and Michael Pillsbury are skating to where the puck is, not where the puck is going.

So where is the puck going? It's important to realize that today we live in an era where we've seen far greater change in thirty years than we've seen in three hundred or even 3,000 years. It's a period of immense change. Future historians will be amazed by what's happened in our era, and everything is still changing. Just to give you one big dimension of how: from the year one to the year 1824—for the last 2,000 years.—the two largest economies in the world were always those of China and India. It's only in the last two hundred years that Europe and

North America took off. So, the past two hundred years of world history have been a major historical aberration. As you know, all aberrations come to a natural end. So it's perfectly natural to see the return of China and India.

So, when you all voted by 76 percent to say that China is a threat to the liberal international order, what you were expressing is a deep gut feeling that China has changed the world, and it has. When China, which had 10 percent of the United States' gross national product [GNP] in PPP [purchasing power parity] terms in 1980, becomes bigger than the United States in 2014—in thirty-four years—everything changes.

But what is China threatening? Is China threatening the liberal international order, or is China threatening the global balance of power and the number-one power in the world, so ably represented by General McMaster and Michael Pillsbury? And the honest answer—there's only one simple, honest answer—is that China is threatening the global balance of power. I'll tell you why China is *not* threatening the liberal international order. Because why has China come out of nowhere and in thirty years become the largest economy in PPP terms? How did China do it? China did it because of the rules of the liberal international order.

Now, many of you will be confused by this phrase, "liberal international order." I could completely agree with what General McMaster and Michael Pillsbury said when they suggested that China is not a liberal *domestic* order, but that's not the issue of the day. The issue of the day is whether China is working with the liberal *international* order. And I can tell you what the liberal international order is because I was born in an era of what you might call an *illiberal* international order, in a British colony. You know, when you're colonized you have no rights whatsoever. China went through a hundred years of hell from 1842 to 1949 and then, when the liberal international order began, China discovered two big things that worked for it. One, the first pillar of the liberal international order is sovereignty. Every country can decide its own future and what it wants to do. And then the second pillar is rules: rules to ensure what you can and cannot do in the international space. Not domestic space, international space.

I also want to give you one statistic that I hope you will bear in mind throughout this whole debate. Of the world's population of 7.5 billion people, only 12 percent live in the West; 88 percent live outside the West. So, you want to judge China's international behaviour — let me emphasize that — *international* behaviour, ask yourself how the 88 percent is reacting to China's rise. Amazingly, they're welcoming it, they're co-operating with it. My partner Henry Wang described what is happening in the Belt and Road Initiative. Countries are queuing up to join it. Of course, the United States doesn't want to join. I understand; why would the United States want to go and support its number-one competitor? It won't. But the rest of the world is doing so.

So, the debate is about the liberal international order; please pay attention to international sentiments. Thank you.

RUDYARD GRIFFITHS: Wow, I think we have a debate here, gentlemen. So we're going to put two and a half minutes up on the clock. We'll do a round of rebuttals and we're going to proceed in the same order of our opening remarks. So, H. R. McMaster, you're up first.

H. R. MCMASTER: Thank you. Well, the negative team would have you believe that we should be happy about Xi Jinping making the world safe for authoritarianism. Today, the way China exports its authoritarian model is to use this program of Belt and Road to indebt nations way beyond what they could ever repay. Thirty-three of those countries have already reached an unsustainable level of debt; eight are already in deep distress. And so what China does is that it undermines the sovereignty of these countries by trying to recreate the tributary system associated with Chinese dynastic history, where you can live in the system only as long as you accept a servile relationship with China at the centre.

Kishore is talking about sovereignty, so he would have us believe, on the thirtieth anniversary of the Tiananmen Square massacre, that the Chinese people really enjoy having no rights and living inside an authoritarian system. It used to be that Kishore only spoke for the four billion people in Asia, but now he's speaking for everybody, except, I guess, North America and the West. How *do* the countries in the region view China's effort to export its authoritarian system? They view it with a great deal of concern, and even fear.

What you've seen recently is a reaction across the

world, where small countries like Sri Lanka who could no longer service their debt voted out the corrupt government that welcomed in this financing and created this servile relationship. A similar phenomenon happened in the Maldives, and it's happened in this hemisphere. Consider, for example, how China is making money on the backs of the Venezuelan people by keeping up the cash flow to Maduro in exchange for all of his oil exports at a discount, which China immediately resells on the international market. The new prime minister of Malaysia, another country subjected to this kind of servile relationship, has said this reminds him of the unequal treaties to which China was subjected in the nineteenth and early twentieth centuries.

So, what you see is this authoritarian model being exported. It is not a U.S.-China or Canada-China problem. It is a competition between our free and open societies and an authoritarian closed system. Thank you.

RUDYARD GRIFFITHS: Okay. Again, we're going to follow the same order as the opening remarks. So Henry, you're up next.

HUIYAO WANG: Thank you. I think that what Mr. McMaster has said may be based on abstract theories and not really fact-driven, at least not in the majority of instances. What I can tell you is that the Belt and Road Initiative has been in progress for the last five years. It's actually brought a lot of benefit to countries around the world. Since the financial crisis we haven't had any major stimulus plans. One of the ambassadors from a developing country told me: "Look, what has the U.S. given us? For the last twenty or thirty years, we haven't got anything really to work on for an international development plan."

China, after four decades of absorbing, learning, and benefiting from all the countries and multinational companies coming in, has developed. So it's time to give back, to really to contribute. Take, for example, Belt and Road. The *Financial Times* has just recently released a report done by the Radian Group, a very famous consulting company based in New York, on all the projects China's done in the last ten years. Of the thirty-eight projects under development in twenty-four countries, fourteen were being written off by China, and in eleven the loan and financing was delayed. There is no hard evidence to support that they're debt traps.

In Kenya, on the railway built by China, it's very difficult to get a train ticket now. The train has really helped the local economy. In Kazakhstan, for the first time in history, they have a train that goes directly to port, through China. And think of the freight between China and the city of Duisburg in Germany. There used to be forty trains a week and now there are a hundred, generating employment opportunities for 6,000 in that German city. There's also the port that China is helping manage in Greece, which used to be ninety-something in the world for container and volume handling, and is now in the top thirty.

So, there are abundant examples of China trying to do good things for the world. Of course, the Belt and Road Initiative is still building. It's been just five years;

it's a long-term project. But let's work together. It's like a venture capital project. China put up the seed money, but let's have an A round, a B round, a C round, and let's make it prosper!

RUDYARD GRIFFITHS: Thank you. Okay, Michael. We're going to put two and a half minutes up on the clock. Go at it.

MICHAEL PILLSBURY: The global liberal international order actually didn't begin in 1945 with the U.N. Charter, and China is not the only threat to it. The order — in the way international relations theory is taught around the world, including in India and Japan, which I'm going to mention in a minute — began in two obscure little towns in Germany in 1638 to end a war that had gone on for thirty years over religion, and in which millions had died. The idea was: First of all, to structure a set of treaties that will invent sovereignty. Second, for there to be a set of rules for how to prevent war from happening among the major powers. And third, that those who would sign had to abide by certain internal rules in their countries. It didn't work. It worked for a long time, but not ultimately. Another set of rules was defined in 1815. Again, to avert war, maintain the order, set up a system for harmonizing differences. It lasted more or less a hundred years. The League of Nations, similar story. America didn't join, China got angry over the arrangements, so it failed.

World War II. There was one last effort, which built on all the previous efforts: the current world order. China, for the first twenty years, as Henry Wang sort of alluded to, was not part of the order. It was kept out as a leper, because of the Korean War and many other reasons. Then China joined, and for more than twenty years took it very seriously. It's only fairly recently, in the past decade or so, that China has shifted toward being this threat, and India and Japan see it too. It's not just Canada and the United States or, more and more, Germany. It's the neighbours.

The Indians have now become the number-two arms purchaser from the United States. They faced a military threat on their border just two years ago. China backed down, ultimately, partly because the Indian forces surrounded what the Chinese were trying to do. We haven't even gone into Japan's reaction or China's massive defence spending on space — outer space weapons, hypersonic weapons — a whole series of things that China once told us, "We will never do that."

KISHORE MAHBUBANI: Let me just make two quick points: First, we don't disagree that China does not have a liberal democratic society. That's not the argument. We agree with you.

MICHAEL PILLSBURY: So, you're going to vote for us?

[laughter from the audience]

KISHORE MAHBUBANI: Yes, China's got lots of problems and challenges, but let me just describe to you one story about the country. When I first went to China in 1980, people couldn't choose what to wear, where to live, where to work, and what to study, and zero Chinese could travel overseas as tourists—zero. Today, when you go to China, you see that the Chinese people can choose what to wear, where to live, where to work, what to study, and each year, in this amazing land of "non-freedom," 134 million Chinese—how many times the population of Canada?—travel overseas freely and, voting with their feet, they come back to China: 134 million every year! What's wrong with them? A hundred and thirty-four million people can't see what's happening in China? Think again.

Second point: the best concept I learned in philosophy is paradox. The paradox of our global situation is that the biggest threat to the liberal international order is not a non-liberal society like China but a liberal society like the United States of America. I consulted two of the leading scholars in America. John Mearsheimer [of the University of Chicago] said, "Kishore, you can go on the stage and tell them that I, John Mearsheimer, believe that the biggest threat to the liberal international order comes from the United States of America and not from China." And if you read John Ikenberry, of Princeton University, he says the liberal international order faces a danger not of murder but of suicide, by its creators. So, think of that.

RUDYARD GRIFFITHS: Gentlemen, a terrific debate so far. We're going to get into the moderated middle of this debate and work through some of the key issues. I want to pick up where Kishore left off and I want to also begin by touching on the news of this last week, where we've seen trade tensions between China and the United States ratchet up considerably.

H. R. McMaster, let me begin with you. Will you level with this audience and admit that this trade dispute is not about defending the liberal international order? It's about pursuing America's narrow security interests by clipping China's wings economically and technologically, and by doing this you're creating huge damage to this critical bilateral relationship, and, more importantly, you're knocking the pins out from under the liberal international order. Doesn't America have something to answer for here?

H. R. MCMASTER: Well, actually, Rudyard, those are the Chinese Communist Party's talking points, right? And I think that what you've seen in the last two years, maybe, is a recognition across all of our free and open societies that the assumptions on which we had based our policy toward China were wrong. Henry mentioned that really we should be proud of China for being part of all these international organizations. Well, it's just too bad that Chinese policies are undermining those very organizations, and that all of the promises made, for example, when joining the WTO were broken. And what were some of these promises? That China would open its market to international companies. Of course, they've done so, but with the proviso that when you come in to do business you transfer all of your intellectual property to Chinese companies that act as an extension of the Chinese Communist Party.

The other aspect of this is that your company has to adhere to and support the foreign policy of the Chinese

Communist Party. You'd better not criticize putting millions of people in concentration camps. You'd better stick to the party's position on Tibet—and you've seen Marriott, you've seen major airlines, being subjected to this kind of coercion. But what you also see with China breaking these trade and economic protocols is China using the coercive power of its market to soften criticism of themselves, because companies want to maintain economic access, even as we in the West have been subjected to a sustained campaign of industrial espionage of unprecedented scale.

Kishore would try to make this a problem between the United States and China, but the people in China are waking up. Why are the wealthiest people of China buying up all of your real estate in Vancouver? They know. They know about the changes that have happened from 2011 on, and they want to get ready to get the hell out of there, or at least get their money the hell out of there. And so we have to recognize China's behaviour.

Now, why are they behaving that way? We can have another conversation about that, but it's because Xi Jinping has prioritized maintaining his grip on power over what makes sense economically, even for the Chinese people. And so, if he's not going to liberalize the economy, it's going to be tough to grow unless you steal other people's intellectual property.

RUDYARD GRIFFITHS: Let me pause there because I want to bring Henry in on that point. Henry, it's clear that the trade deal has gotten held up this week largely because

China's leadership does not want, it seems, to give its control of the economy over to the market mechanisms that the United States has been promoting — so an end of forced technology transfer, an end of subsidies to state-owned corporations. Aren't those cornerstones of the liberal international order? Aren't those principles that are embedded in the WTO that China is already a signatory to? Why has China resisted these market reforms, seemingly ratcheting the tension about these negotiations up to a whole new level?

HUIYAO WANG: I can't really agree with what Mr. McMaster has been describing. I think the narrative in the West has really been a little bit overdone, actually. You know, since joining the WTO, China has greatly embraced the global treaty system. Of course, there are certain requirements, certain conditions for joining, and there's a review by the WTO every year, and China is a good student. China really is.

China has developed through the WTO. So, if China has developed in ways that are not allowed by the WTO, let's reform the WTO, not act unilaterally against China for all the reasons talked about. For example, there's a lot of talk about China's theft and China's forced technology transfer. Maybe people want to talk about joint ventures, but joint ventures are allowed under the WTO's conditions.

And there's no hard evidence. So far, I haven't seen any real cases, any examples, of companies that have been forced into technology transfers. As a matter of fact, last March, China swiftly passed a new foreign investment law that stipulates no forced technology transfer by any government at any level. No intellectual property stealing by any company. If it does so, it will be prosecuted. It will be punished.

So I think your question is right. At this critical moment, maybe there are cultural issues, but why can't we just continue negotiations? I mean, China needs this deal, the U.S. needs the deal, the business community, all of the world needs the deal. We don't want uncertainty. If the two largest economies fight each other, all the rest of the world's going to suffer.

So, I think it's really up to the leadership, I think particularly the U.S. right now. Let's not effect a tariff. At midnight tonight, President Trump will launch a 25 percent tariff on China. But you know what? Fifty percent of those exports out of China were done by your American companies. GM and Ford sell more cars in China than in the United States. China's the second-largest market for Apple. And Walmart purchased 30 percent of its products from China to supply thousands of U.S. supermarkets.

If there's 25 percent added to costs, that's added to the American consumers. Americans are paying that. The stock market is really reflecting that now. We don't want that kind of uncertainty, so let's solve this. Let's have cool heads. Let's think about the U.S. and China. Let's think about the world. Let's demonstrate our leadership to the world.

RUDYARD GRIFFITHS: I'm going to Kishore and then Michael to weigh in on why these trade talks have blown up. Kishore, how do you wrap what we've seen this week around this debate on the future of the liberal international order?

KISHORE MAHBUBANI: Well, let's state the obvious: the dispute is not about trade. Trade is just the arena where they are fighting. But it was inevitable. When China's GNP became so big, and in PPP terms it became bigger than the United States', the United States felt uncomfortable, felt threatened, and had to hit back. And this is what all great powers do, right? It's rational behaviour on the part of the United States to thwart a rising competitor. But this is a battle between the United States and China — and believe me, be careful with the facts you get. Trust me. A lot of it is propaganda. You do not know what's real. You don't know what's going on. One day they're fighting, next day they smile, they shake hands, and they make a deal, right? We don't know what's really going on.

So this is my advice to people outside, to the Canadians, Singaporeans, and the rest of the world — remember the wisdom in an old Sri Lankan proverb: "When elephants fight, the grass suffers; when elephants make love, the grass also suffers."

RUDYARD GRIFFITHS: So, Michael, you've been an advisor to President Trump on his China strategy. Many people would say this is an example of American unilateralism. Here in Canada we certainly know what that unilateralism feels like in terms of the trade deal that we were required to sign. A trade deal that, as a point of fact, I'm sure you're aware, precludes Canada not only from entering into a

trade agreement with China but from even having negotiations with Beijing. So how is that in favour or in support
of the values and principles that you so eloquently speak
for in terms of the liberal international order?

H. R. MCMASTER: It was Pillsbury's idea to put that in.

[laughter from the audience]

MICHAEL PILLSBURY: I think I can explain. I can explain
President Trump's trade strategy if that interests you, but
I'm more interested in the idea of whether the elephants
fight or the elephants make love, because Kishore has
got a very important point here. When China and the
United States, or other great powers, or even the smallest
countries in the world, have grown too close together in
the past, that affects everybody because of the so-called
G2, put forward by one of your predecessors, Zbigniew
Brzezinski, my teacher at Columbia. The idea of the G2
is that all the main issues can pretty much be solved by
the two great powers, great economies, and the others
can just take it.

That vision is still alive in Washington, D.C. In fact,
if you look at the president's comments about the end
of the trade war, he wants zero tariffs between the U.S.
and China. He wants more U.S. investment in China. His
commerce secretary has welcomed Chinese investment
other than in sensitive national security sectors, but in
everything else. He's had trade shows to attract more
Chinese investors. So the G2 vision, the elephants making

love, I think that has to be kept in mind if China stops threatening the global international order.

Now, as for the elephants fighting, that's also an important scenario. Both countries have begun to hold war games and military exercises, write books, give speeches about war between the two countries. This is also bad because again, Kissinger's book *On China*—by the way, my book has now outsold him, so I can afford to praise his book—talks about a major war coming between the U.S. and China on the scale of World War I. Millions will die. So I'd rather have the elephants make love than fight each other.

RUDYARD GRIFFITHS: Let's go to the military dimension of this debate. I'm going to have to start with the general in the room here and ask you: Aren't the Chinese really the persistent victims of U.S. aggression? I mean, just this week, in the heat of these trade negotiations, your navy decides to sail two destroyers armed to the gills through the South China Sea without even asking. Regardless of whether you debate whether they own the South China Sea, you didn't even ask permission. You know, last time I looked, I didn't see the Chinese navy sitting off Staten Island.

MICHAEL PILLSBURY: You *will*!

[laughter from the audience]

RUDYARD GRIFFITHS: Explain to this audience how it is that, while China shows restraint, the U.S. projects aggression.

H. R. MCMASTER: So China is showing restraint by building islands in the South China Sea—destroying an ecosystem, by the way, as they're doing it—and militarizing those islands against international law and against an international court ruling? What China is doing is laying claim to the ocean, and not just any ocean but a part of the ocean through which one-fifth of global trade flows. And, as Henry said, China has benefited from the liberal international order. It adheres to international law and recognizes that nobody owns the ocean, nobody has to ask anybody's permission to execute global commerce. But this is what China is trying to put into place. Now, why are they doing that?

They're doing that because what China wants to do—and this is explicit in Document No. 9, which Henry can't even talk about because he'd probably be detained when he got back to China—is create exclusionary areas of control, of primacy, that they can push the United States out of. Why? Because without the United States you can intimidate countries like Singapore. And I'd like to ask Kishore: I wonder how your government feels about you being an apologist for the Chinese Communist Party's policies in the region, because when I talk to Singaporean officials, they sound much different than you do.

And so what we have to recognize is that it is time to have a conversation with China, to explain to China that its activities to establish hegemonic control over the

Indo-Pacific region and to challenge the United States, Canada — any free and open societies and what we stand for globally — has got to stop. And China — and Xi Jinping and, really, the Chinese Communist Party — has to recognize that China is risking all those tremendous gains that Kishore listed, the lifting of hundreds of millions of people out of poverty. All that is in jeopardy now, and so it's not just a military issue. All of these issues are integrated.

I just would like to say something quickly: Kishore and Henry said, well, you know, everybody *loves* the Belt and Road. Well, let's ask a country in our hemisphere, Ecuador, how's that's going for them. A $2.6 billion dam built at the base of an active volcano, whose turbines were clogged immediately by trees and silt. The first time it was cranked up it blew out the entire country's electrical system. All of the officials who were involved in that deal — guess where they are? They're in jail, because what China uses is corruption in this campaign of co-option and, ultimately, coercion. And what does Ecuador get in return now? It gives up all of its oil exports to China, which China then immediately sells at a markup on the global market.

That's what China's system looks like. Land grabs, so to speak, in the South China Sea that restrict international commerce, and creating servile relationships and dependencies with authoritarian corrupt regimes, so that it can challenge our free and open societies and international order.

RUDYARD GRIFFITHS: I want to let Kishore respond here. A direct charge of sorts was levelled against you, Kishore, that you are an apologist for the Chinese government. So let's have you address that, and more broadly, let's stay on the topic of the military security component of this debate, because the general's just set out a litany of charges here that I'd like a response to.

KISHORE MAHBUBANI: First of all, thank you, General McMaster, for confirming that I'm not speaking on behalf of the Singapore government. Yes, as an academic, I think my job is to just tell the truth, and you can decide later on whether or not what I've said is factually correct or factually incorrect. That's the only standard by which I ask to be judged; if it happens to agree with the American position or the Chinese position, it all depends on whether or not it's true.

So let me just state two facts for you on the military dimension. First, you know, the only major power on Planet Earth that actually hasn't gone to war in forty years, hasn't fired one bullet in thirty years across its borders, is China. By contrast, under the peaceful presidency of Barack Obama in the last year of his administration, the United States dropped 26,000 bombs on seven countries. Now, these are facts. Am I being an apologist for the Chinese government? Go and check the facts.

Now, fact number two will be even more interesting to you because, technically, I'm afraid it may be a secret. When I served as non-resident high commissioner to Canada, a very senior Canadian diplomat told me an amazing story. He said that for many years in the north of Canada there was a dispute between the United States and Canada as to whether a body of water was an internal waterway of Canada or was an international strait under the United Nations Convention on the Law of the Sea. Canada said, no, it's an internal waterway. United States said, no, no, it's international waters. And so the dispute carries on and the Canadians were busy writing papers to prove their case, and then the United States responded by sending a destroyer through the straits.

Now, by the way, under international law, you are allowed to shoot a destroyer in your internal waters, but you wisely decided not to do so. You are very wise, very wise. You could have taken the United States to the World Court. Many countries took the United States to the World Court and the United States just ignored the rulings. You know that, right?

The most recent ruling, by the way, is on an island occupied by the United States and the U.K. in the Indian Ocean, which the World Court has ruled belongs to Mauritius, but it's still occupied by the U.S. and the U.K. and has not been given up. So, I think, if the United States set an example of obeying international law, then I think that would be the best way to persuade China to abide by international law.

H. R. MCMASTER: Okay, just a quick point. First of all, I'd like to applaud Kishore's effort to make this debate about something else, but what I would like to do is to point out—

KISHORE MAHBUBANI: Just facts. Just facts.

H. R. MCMASTER: — is to just point out that a good percentage of those bombs that the United States dropped were in support of allied and Canadian soldiers who were courageously fighting alongside us against the enemies of all civilizations.

RUDYARD GRIFFITHS: I want to move on. We've got a number of topics that I want to get through in this portion of the debate, and the next has to be human rights. Michael, I want to come to you because in your opening remarks you talked about this larger kind of call to arms to a world where individual rights are respected, where individual freedoms thrive. But how can you refute the fact that China cares about human rights, and that not only do they care about them but it's shown in what they've accomplished? It's shown in what Henry and Kishore have talked about, 800 million people lifted out of poverty. An incredible accomplishment by any nation or any civilization. How can you say that caring about basic human rights is less important than, say, caring about the rights that *you* might like — freedom of the press, the right to academic freedom? Don't those seem kind of secondary in a country like China that faces these urgent social problems?

MICHAEL PILLSBURY: Well, let me tell you a story. There were a couple of Communist Party leaders of China. They both got fired and they both went to jail. They said, "Yes, basic human rights are good. We need to bring as many as we can out of poverty," and they succeeded. But they also stuck up not only for human rights as I define them but also for the rule of law, elections. They translated James Madison into a draft constitution for China. Nobody knew this at the time. This was all in the 1980s. We learned it because the second of the two party secretaries who went to jail for life wrote his memoirs, and he described how far things had gone in China in the '80s toward the rule of law, open elections, a multi-party system. And I emphasize, where did he spend the rest of his life? House arrest, prison. It was only much later that we learned about this internal debate.

So yes, China knows about basic human rights and has had great success in the sense of elevating people out of poverty. I think it's China's greatest achievement of all. But the reformers also know about the other part of your question, and that's where this tragedy is taking us. The trends are heading in the wrong direction in China because of this power struggle back in 2011 and 2012. The question now is, is it hopeless? Is China on the wrong path? Are we going either to war or toward a sort of global surveillance technology system that they want to export to the whole world, whereby you, Rudyard, will be evaluated by which magazines you subscribe to, what kind of food you buy, what you said, surreptitiously perhaps, to someone else, and so your credit card score—it's called a social credit system—will then designate how you should be treated the next time you go to the Canadian government. I don't think you want that. That's what China stands for now.

This wasn't the case ten or twenty years ago. It's something new. It's going to compromise the human rights of the whole world if they're not called on this and asked to stop.

RUDYARD GRIFFITHS: Let me bring Kishore and Henry in on this, because this is key. People in this room and your opponents here would like to frame this debate as a contest not just between variations of the liberal order but as something much more dangerous, potentially, which is a contest between freedom and despotism. Is that a fair way to characterize this debate?

HUIYAO WANG: Well, I don't think that that is really a fair way to characterize the argument because, you see, China actually has its own situation. China has a 5,000-year history and 1.4 billion people, still the largest population in the world. So, to govern and manage a population like that, with people in different regions, is really a big challenge. I think China has to uphold human rights, of course, but it also has the right to development. But look, China has embraced the market economy. The market economy is actually, you know, a democratic economy. People vote with the wallet for everything. Now they don't even have to use a wallet; they use their mobile phone. What to buy, where to go, what to do — basically, you exercise your vote in everything.

China has one billion smartphone users and has become a cashless society. So, in that sense, China has come really a long way. I don't think China has reached the status of a developed country yet, but to its credit it now has compulsory education for 200 million students, up to nine years, and also a basic medical care for the whole country, almost like Canada—probably more than the United States. So, I think this is actually a great achievement.

Also, the people are developing the high-speed train network. This Chinese New Year I had relatives coming from Hangzhou, from their village there. Four hours, five hours to Beijing. So convenient. You just take the train and come say hello to me. So, you can imagine the big transport system now, all the infrastructure there.

China has more assets than the United States. China wants peace now. It's absolutely important for China to keep the peace and to support, enhance, and improve the liberal international order for China's benefit and for the benefit of the U.S. and the rest of the world.

RUDYARD GRIFFITHS: Kishore, come in on this. Your opponents are saying that your division in this debate between the international liberal order as a global phenomenon and domestic politics is a false one, because the domestic dimension informs international behaviour and action. Why do you refute that?

KISHORE MAHBUBANI: Well, I think the trouble about such a debate is that you always end up with black and white perspectives, and you lose the nuances. So it is a fact—I mean, I completely agree with General McMaster and Michael Pillsbury—that the standards for human rights in the United States are much higher than those in China.

It's a fact: you have freedom of speech, you get freedom to riot and so on, so forth. And clearly, China is a long way away. But the other question for us is, which society is progressing and which society is regressing? And let me just give you three important facts about regression. Fact number one: the only major developed society where the average income of the bottom 50 percent has gone *down* over the past thirty years is the United States of America. Fact number two — and I mention this in my book *Has the West Lost It?* — two-thirds, *two-thirds*, of American households don't have $500 cash for emergency purposes. I think two-thirds of Chinese households may have got there already.

Fact number three — and this is the most damaging fact: When I studied philosophy at Dalhousie University in 1974–75, if anyone had said to me, "Kishore, in the future, the first major developed Western country to reintroduce torture will be the United States of America," I would have taken a bet with them 1,000 to one that would *never* happen in my lifetime. Believe me, it was a great personal shock to me when Guantanamo happened. How is it that the world's biggest defender of human rights became the first major developed country to reintroduce torture, and, amazingly enough, a Canadian citizen was taken, I believe, from New York to Syria to be tortured.

Now, I would like to live in a world where there's zero torture and, if we can work together to achieve that world and have there be no torture anywhere in the world, let's work together for that.

H. R. MCMASTER: Of course, nobody says that any of our societies are flawless, right? But when we do discover flaws in our government's behaviour, we debate them, they get exposed, and we are self-critical and we improve. Imagine, could we even have this debate in Beijing?

And I would also ask how many people are trying to become Chinese citizens? There's a reason. There's a reason for that great disparity between those who want to come to free and open societies and those who prefer not to live in authoritarian, closed, police surveillance states.

HUIYAO WANG: Actually, there's one new development. Last year, China set up a new semi-ministerial-level organization, a national immigration administration. Now there are more foreigners coming to China. China issued over 2,000 green cards last year. So, China's learning from the United States now. HSBC has released a report for expatriates working overseas. China's one of the top most attractive countries to work for. So I think there are also opportunities there.

RUDYARD GRIFFITHS: Two-way trade.

MICHAEL PILLSBURY: Well, and thanks to the one-child policy, you do need some young labour as well.

RUDYARD GRIFFITHS: Let's move on to two more topics I want to touch on before we go to our closing statements. The first is technology, because this has been a big feature not only of these ongoing trade negotiations but also of this increasing rivalry between China and the United States and the rest of the Western world. Who has the technological competitive advantage?

H. R. McMaster, you were in the White House. You served as national security advisor. Why is the United States, some would say, bullying its allies into removing the Huawei 5G technology from their networks when the United States doesn't even have a 5G technology to sell to these countries? And we know that through your NSA [National Security Agency] you're spying on all of us anyway. I mean, come on. This looks like the pot calling the kettle black.

H. R. MCMASTER: What China is doing is engaging in a systemic campaign of industrial espionage to steal sensitive technologies and intellectual property and apply it not only to their efforts to dominate key sectors of the emerging global economy but also to an unprecedented military buildup. In 2015 when President Xi Jinping visited the Rose Garden with President Obama, he said, "We promise we're not going to do that anymore." But what China did is that they just shifted that espionage effort— or large portions of it—over into the private sector and produced a law that said, if you're a Chinese company you have to support our intelligence collection efforts. Why would anyone in their right mind let China establish your communications infrastructure if you know that this authoritarian police state is going to collect all of your data, label that data, and try to use it against you later?

Hundreds of thousands of records of federal

employees have been transferred essentially to the Chinese Communist Party. China Telecom already owns the ten really big communications hubs in North America. The Chinese Communist Party already has access to communications between the U.S. and Canada by controlling those hubs. And so it's just irresponsible, I think, on the part of any government, to let the Chinese Communist Party into their systems. If the Chinese Communist Party treats its own people the way it does, do you think they're going to treat you any better? I don't think so.

So, the extinguishment of privacy, globally, is what China is endeavouring to do by the establishment of this infrastructure.

KISHORE MAHBUBANI: I think the key issue here is surveillance and spying and I completely agree with General McMaster that it is wrong. One story and one point. I was in Vancouver a few weeks ago—not to buy a property but to participate in a TED Talk. But the most powerful speaker at the TED Talk was a British journalist called Carole Cadwalladr—if you ever watch a TED Talk, watch hers—and she describes graphically how Facebook, as she says, "destroyed British democracy." How? By injecting lies into Facebook accounts that enter and disappear without a trace. It took months and months before the British Parliament could actually see the lies that Facebook had fed. So, what's the solution?

The solution to the problems of Facebook, Huawei, or any such corporation is to create an open set of multilateral rules agreed to by all countries—that's what the liberal international order is about — and to say, this is what is acceptable in cyberwarfare and this is what is unacceptable in cyberwarfare. And I can say confidently that the number-one country that will oppose this will be the United States of America, because the United States of America has by far the best surveillance capability of any country in the world. The number-one country is the United States, number two is Russia, number three and four are Israel and the United Kingdom, and number five is China. And that's the reason why the Chinese get caught, because they're so bad at it!

RUDYARD GRIFFITHS: Let's move on to the last topic for this free-for-all and then we'll go to closing statements. This debate is originating in Toronto, in Canada, and I want to go around the horn here and get this distinguished group's advice. When the elephants are either making war or making love, what do smaller powers like Canada, like Singapore, do? What is the strategy to, let's hope thrive, but maybe simply to survive this superpower rivalry? Michael, let's start with you.

MICHAEL PILLSBURY: Well, small powers, as you phrase it, can have an enormous amount of influence when they gather together in a coalition in one of the organizations that does this. The most important is the U.N. General Assembly. There have been efforts to declare that the U.S. practises torture or does surveillance. If you do a kind of a test count in the U.N. General Assembly on that, it won't pass. That's why, by the way, I praise

Lester Pearson for his role in the shaping of the U.N. Charter in 1945 and his almost-time as secretary-general of the U.N.

The U.N. structure itself is probably the most important part of the global international order. It includes arms-control treaties. And Canada has also played an important role in getting the two powers of the Soviet Union — Russia — and the United States to have bilateral nuclear arms-control treaties. There are a number of successes. China has just destroyed one of the most important arms-control treaties that there ever was. It's a treaty on so-called intermediate nuclear missiles of a certain range. We and the Russians would destroy them completely. We had teams in each other's factories to make sure nobody built missiles like that. Everything was fine and then China began to deploy missiles, thousands of them, in just that range, causing both Russia, which has concerns and even fears about the Chinese military, and us to withdraw from the treaty. It caused the Russians, in response to these Chinese nuclear missiles, to even say, "We are now going to place more emphasis on nuclear forces than ever before so we'll have some kind of countermeasure to what China's doing."

Recently, the American side asked China, "Could you join us in three-way talks with Russia, China, and America to reduce those missiles and all the others, because soon the entire arms-control agreement on ICBMs [intercontinental ballistic missiles] will expire? Can you also reduce defence spending? Help us reduce defence spending in all three capitals." China gave its answer yesterday. "No. No."

So that's a spoiler in the international system that really worries me a lot.

RUDYARD GRIFFITHS: So what's Canada's strategy?

MICHAEL PILLSBURY: Canada could help with that. Canada could say, we like this idea of three-way talks. China, why don't you get on board?

H. R. MCMASTER: Well, I think what Kishore's tried to set up is really a false debate here about China versus the United States, and everybody in between gets trampled. This is really an issue between free and open societies and closed authoritarian systems and, despite the narrative of unilateralism, there's been tremendous multinational co-operation on confronting the predatory and dangerous policies of the Chinese Communist Party.

So just consider, for example, the bad effects of the Belt and Road Initiative and how that's creating these debt dependencies and failed projects and bolstering corrupt authoritarian regimes from Venezuela to Cambodia to Zimbabwe. What the United States has done is to work together with Canada, Japan, Australia, and New Zealand to say that there have to be some standards. Kishore said it's important to have standards. And so now we are establishing standards that can help reduce the threat of Belt and Road to these other countries. And we're also putting our money together so that there are financial alternatives to the predatory policies of the Chinese Communist Party.

Henry mentioned the AIIB as funding some of these projects. Very few projects are funded by the AIIB because Canada and others sit on its board and they won't conscience the funding of these corrupt projects in corrupt governments.

Another example is that on December 20, 2018, Canada was at the vanguard with sixteen other countries who simultaneously exposed the systematic campaign of industrial espionage that's affected by so-called APT10 hacking attacks. All nations announced at the same time a range of sanctions and indictments against the individuals that were engaged in that espionage that President Xi had promised they would never do again.

And again, don't let Kishore trick us into thinking that this is about the United States and China. The European Commission last month officially recognized China as a systematic rival promoting alternative models of governance.

Also, there have been recent media exposures where U.S. and Canadian investigative journalists have worked together to expose how the Chinese Communist Party has allowed this drug fentanyl, this murderous drug, to be exported without any kind of checks into both of our countries—and by the way, the per capita death rate in Canada is even higher than the massive death rate in the United States. And so investigative journalists, not just governments, play a very, very important role in exposing the activities and efforts of the Chinese Communist Party to export its authoritarian model.

RUDYARD GRIFFITHS: Kishore, you've heard the laundry list.

KISHORE MAHBUBANI: Yes. You know, as a student of philosophy I would say neither of them answered your question. Your question was, "What do small states do?" and they didn't answer the question. They went on and gave their speeches.

The question was: What should small states do? And the answer is that you ask states like Canada and Singapore—and by the way, if you take the 193 member states of the U.N. and take away China and the U.S., there are 191 still there—you ask these 191 states what they would like. They would like a stronger United Nations, they would like stronger international law, and they would like things to be adjudicated by impartial bodies and not sort of unilateral demands made by one superpower on the other countries.

I know, because I read American papers, that when General McMaster was the national security advisor he fought a very noble fight. He tried very hard to persuade President Trump not to walk away from multilateral agreements, not to walk away from the Paris Climate Accord, not to walk away from the Trans-Pacific Partnership. Guess what happened? He failed. And that's the sad story. When you have an honourable man like him trying to do the right thing and he fails, you have to ask yourself the question: How do you live in a world when a superpower decides to walk away from multilateral agreements?

So the answer to that I can tell you. I served as

ambassador to the U.N. for ten years, and in the course of ten years I've spoken with some degree of intensity with ambassadors from Africa, from Latin America and elsewhere, and the one thing we all agree upon when we sit together is, "Let's try to strengthen the U.N. and make it the place where you can go impartially." The only protection that medium powers like Canada and small states like Singapore have is a stronger multilateral order, and I hope that General McMaster will get back into the U.S. government and win the fight the next time.

RUDYARD GRIFFITHS: Henry?

HUIYAO WANG: Thank you. I think the debate tonight is very meaningful. I think that we are at a crossroads for the global liberal international order. You know, for the last seventy-five years, since after World War II, we haven't seen any major wars, a third world war, because we have this new liberal international order. So, let's maintain it. I think that Canada is a great country. Canada not long ago had WTO meetings — China and the U.S. were not there — and I think Canada can play an enormous role as a G7 country. Canada really has a unique role in a neutral position to do this kind of thing.

So I think it's really important for Canadian people to speak out. And Canada is very international. You have a multicultural system. You know, you have English and French and everybody gets along very well.

RUDYARD GRIFFITHS: Most of the time.

HUIYAO WANG: At least Quebec is still in Canada, right?

I think that in the past seven decades, the world has fundamentally changed. We're so intertwined. We're so interconnected. The movement of capital, the movement of goods, the movement of talent, migration: we are actually one world, one dream. We cannot separate from each other. Let's be realistic. Let's not shake up this multilateral system. Let's multilateralize, including with Belt and Road. Let China and the U.S. work together for a multilateral Belt and Road. Let's make it more responsible for all the countries.

I think that the world needs us and that we cannot really leave the multilateral system. The liberal international order should be strengthened, maintained, and China can be a new contributor to this system.

RUDYARD GRIFFITHS: Great, thank you. That ends our time for the cross-examination portion. We're now going to go to our closing statements. We're going to put three minutes on the clock and we're going to go in the reverse order of the opening statements. So, Kishore, you're up first.

KISHORE MAHBUBANI: As you can see, this has been a fascinating debate, but I want to emphasize one thing: it's not about fun and games. We are at a very special moment in history when we have a rather narrow window of opportunity to create a better world for tomorrow. And what is this narrow window of opportunity? It is this: that China while it is still number two, not yet fully number one, is prepared to accept the constraints of the liberal international order.

China abides by the major agreements and, when you work with China in the United Nations, as many of us have done, you see they try to support the U.N. all the time. And I can say after ten years in the U.N., that the objective of the United States mission to the U.N. was to weaken it, control its budget, refuse to give it freedom to grow, and when I served as a commissioner to the IAEA [International Atomic Energy Agency], the United States was even trying to strangle them. China, by contrast, was prepared to give more to the U.N., and China is the single biggest contributor of peacekeepers to the United Nations.

So, what is this window of opportunity? While it is still number two, while it is still willing to play by the rules, this is the moment for the United States to actually work with China and to strengthen the multilateral order and to serve as a good role model. Unfortunately, as you know, the United States is doing the opposite. It's walking away from the Paris Climate Agreement, it's withdrawn from UNESCO, it's walked away from the Trans-Pacific Partnership, it's withdrawn from the United Nations Human Rights Council, and I can keep going on and on. And the sad part of all this is that the United States today is creating so many major loopholes in international law, loopholes that China will walk through tomorrow when it becomes number one.

So, if General McMaster and Professor Michael Pillsbury want to preserve this order, the best way to do it is to show China: yes, we'll support you in making the liberal international order a stronger one. Thank you.

RUDYARD GRIFFITHS: Thank you, Kishore, for a great debate performance. Michael, your closing statement, please. We've got your three minutes up on the clock.

MICHAEL PILLSBURY: Thank you. It seems to me that threatening the global international order may come down to just one thing: cheating. You know, in your own relationships or in organizations you belong to or companies you work for, if you embezzle, if you lie, if you cheat, there's a punishment for it. In international politics, since the agreement four hundred years ago I mentioned, there's no punishment for a country that cheats. It's only the moral authority of the other powers that can try to persuade that country to change its ways. Let me give you a couple of examples we haven't mentioned so far that have concerned cheating, why the trade decision tonight one minute after midnight may be so important to China.

In the WTO China was sued by the United States. Other countries joined us. The Chinese market was closed to all foreign credit cards, in particular American credit cards. The dispute-settlement mechanism is to take a vote. The judges voted against China. China acknowledged that they had lost. They said they would now open their market to foreign credit cards — this was in 2012. They never did it, and during that period they had a secret sort of plan to boost their own credit card so that today it's the world's largest by revenue internationally because all the other markets opened themselves to the Chinese credit card. That's cheating. The issue of the trade talks, the issue of technology, is not about America First or does America torture people more than China? That's an unusual competition I don't even know how to address. The issue is, is deception okay? Is cheating okay? Is it okay to join United Nations agencies? Interpol would be a good example. When the Chinese headed Interpol, a huge prestigious achievement for China, the head was suddenly called home, put in jail, with no process. The head of an international agency is treated like a common criminal without even charges, other than that his wife talked to the press.

Faced with this kind of challenge to the liberal international order, what should we do? Should we be quiet and be happy? Should we make love with China? Should we get into a war? Or should we just try to bring this to their attention by putting on tariffs, which we know work? These are not the kind of tariffs that protect America. These tariffs are to bring China to the table to answer for cheating.

RUDYARD GRIFFITHS: Henry, your closing remarks, please.

HUIYAO WANG: Thank you. Tonight has been very memorable. In this famous Roy Thomson Hall we had a debate about international liberal order, of which I think China is still a student, but we have learned a lot. I think this debate will be in my memory for a long time because I learned a lot.

I really admire Canada and the Canadian people. You know, in my high school I heard many times the story of Norman Bethune, the Canadian doctor who sacrificed for China. In my university days, I had a professor who also came from Canada, from Toronto, and taught me for two years. So, ever since the first day I came to Toronto to study at U of T, I have really thought Canada's spirit can play an important role in the future.

I think that, you know, the world is so complex. The world is so colourful. Let's have different models, different practices, and different healthy competition — corporate rivalry, not strategic rivalry. And actually, I think that China's opened up. We give great credit to Deng Xiaoping, and he has a very fundamental and well-remembered saying: "It doesn't matter if it is a white cat or a black cat, as long as it catches mice."

Now we see China is really developing to become the second-largest economy and the largest market in the world. So let's give China a little more space. Let China continue to open up and reform, and then China will really be a great market for the world. As of a matter of fact, Tim Hortons, a Canadian-founded company, just opened its shops in China, and in three years' time they're going to open 1,000 of them in different cities. Starbucks has 3,600 shops across China, in 150 cities. There are 3,000 McDonald's in China. Thomas Friedman, the author of *The World Is Flat*, said that if a country's middle class is growing large enough and they are interested in

McDonald's, if their kids go to McDonald's, they will be less interested in war; they'll be more interested in peace. Who would like to sacrifice such a good life, a prosperous life?

So, I think that we really need to think hard. We are all living on this planet. We have only one Earth. So let's really talk to each other, communicate with each other. Let's not deepen the negative narrative. I think there's a lot of myths about China. Let's look at China; seeing is believing. We have a lot of work to do. Tonight at midnight the 25 percent tariff starts. They are not really moving us in a good direction. Let's work together. Let's solve things for the peace and the prosperity of mankind. Thank you very much.

H. R. MCMASTER: Kishore really pulled out all the stops when he tried to make this about President Trump, right? As you all know, President Trump would love to have his name in any venue. But he's probably disappointed to hear this debate's not about him. This debate is about how our free and open societies are under attack by an authoritarian closed model — a model that is not only affecting the Chinese people by the extinguishment of their rights, their rights to free speech, their rights to privacy, but is also affecting other nations of the world, including our own.

Ask your two Canadian citizens who were essentially taken hostage and are still in captivity, one of them a former diplomat whose child was just born a few weeks ago. The Chinese Communist Party every day exposes the nature of their system, and it's time for us to wake up to it. What Kishore would want to do is create a crisis of confidence in ourselves so that we are no longer able to stand up to this kind of behaviour and the exporting of this authoritarian system to other nations, and the intimidation of other nations to create vassal states and servile relationships. But we ought to vote tonight for our own self-respect, our own self-respect as free and open societies who will no longer, as my colleague Michael said, allow China to cheat, will no longer allow China to export its authoritarian system to others.

When Kishore was in his twenties, Mao Zedong killed fifty million of his own people and then, to keep himself in power, he killed millions more. At that time, Mao decided that he was also going to try to export this revolutionary model to other countries. Xi Jinping has put back into place very tight control of the party. The new vanguard of the Chinese Communist Party now, though, are party officials in suits carrying duffle bags of cash to corrupt governments in an effort to extend their influence and establish exclusionary areas of control; in an effort to intimidate us and others while they regard their behaviour and the threat they pose to our free and open societies as just a normal way of doing business.

It's time tonight to send a very clear message that can allow us to escape this false dilemma between being passive about this problem and war. What we need to do is have a conversation. Thank you.

RUDYARD GRIFFITHS: Debaters, on behalf of a grateful audience, I just want to thank you for tackling some hard issues, for bringing some new insights to an issue that will no doubt inform the national conversation here in Canada and also the global conversation for many years to come. So, ladies and gentlemen, our debaters. Thank you.

And again, I just want to recognize the Peter and Melanie Munk Foundation and the terrific support they've provided for us to all gather together and have this enriching conversation of the mind. So, thank you to the foundation and the Munk family.

Well, here's the moment that we have all been waiting for: our opportunity to vote a second time on tonight's motion, to figure out which one of these two teams has been able to sway opinion in this hall over to their side.

Let's also just for a moment review our pre-debate votes. The initial vote was: 76 percent in favour of the motion, 24 percent opposed. We then asked how many of you were open to changing your mind. That was a pretty big number: 83 percent versus 17 percent. So, let's now see the final results.

Summary: The pre-debate vote was 76 percent in favour of the motion, 24 percent opposed. The final vote showed 74 percent in favour, 26 percent opposed. Given that more voters shifted to the team against the motion, the victory goes to Kishore Mahbubani and Huiyao Wang.

ACKNOWLEDGEMENTS

The Munk Debates are the product of the public-spiritedness of a remarkable group of civic-minded organizations and individuals. First and foremost, these debates would not be possible without the vision and leadership of the Aurea Foundation. Founded in 2006 by Peter and Melanie Munk, the Aurea Foundation supports Canadian individuals and institutions involved in the study and development of public policy. The debates are the foundation's signature initiative, a model for the kind of substantive public policy conversation Canadians can foster globally. Since the creation of the debates in 2008, the foundation has underwritten the entire cost of each semi-annual event. The debates have also benefited from the input and advice of members of the board of the foundation, including Mark Cameron, Andrew Coyne, Devon Cross, Allan Gotlieb, Margaret MacMillan, Anthony Munk, Robert Prichard, and Janice Stein.

For her contribution to the preliminary edit of the book, the debate organizers would like to thank Jane McWhinney.

Since their inception, the Munk Debates have sought to take the discussions that happen at each event to national and international audiences. Here the debates have benefited immeasurably from a partnership with Canada's national newspaper, the *Globe and Mail*, and the counsel of its editor-in-chief, David Walmsley.

With the publication of this superb book, House of Anansi Press is helping the debates reach new audiences in Canada and around the world. The debates' organizers would like to thank Anansi chair Scott Griffin and president and publisher Sarah MacLachlan for their enthusiasm for this book project and insights into how to translate the spoken debate into a powerful written intellectual exchange.

ABOUT THE DEBATERS

H. R. MCMASTER was assistant to the American president for national security affairs and is currently a senior fellow at the Hoover Institution. He holds a Ph.D. in military history, was called one of the world's most influential people by *Time* magazine, and has authored the bestselling book *Dereliction of Duty: Lyndon Johnson, Robert McNamara, the Joint Chiefs of Staff and the Lies That Led to Vietnam.*

MICHAEL PILLSBURY is the director of the Center on Chinese Strategy at the Hudson Institute in Washington, D.C. Hailed as a leading authority on China, Pillsbury is a key advisor to the U.S. government on relations with China. He holds a doctorate from Columbia University, has held senior roles at the U.N. and RAND Corporation, and is the author of *The Hundred-Year Marathon: China's Secret Strategy to Replace America as the Global Superpower.*

KISHORE MAHBUBANI is senior advisor and public policy professor at the National University of Singapore. As a senior diplomat for Singapore, he has held postings in Cambodia, Malaysia, the U.S., and at the U.N, where he served as president of the Security Council. He has authored seven books, including *Has the West Lost It?: A Provocation.*

HUIYAO WANG is the founder and president of one of China's leading independent think tanks, the Center for China and Globalization. He holds a Ph.D. in international business and management from Western University and the University of Manchester and was a senior fellow at Harvard's Kennedy School and the Asia Pacific Foundation of Canada. He has published and edited extensively and was named one of 2018's most influential people by *Newsweek* in China.

ABOUT THE EDITOR

RUDYARD GRIFFITHS is the chair of the Munk Debates and president of the Aurea Charitable Foundation. In 2006 he was named one of Canada's "Top 40 under 40" by the *Globe and Mail*. He is the editor of thirteen books on history, politics, and international affairs, including *Who We Are: A Citizen's Manifesto*, which was a *Globe and Mail* Best Book of 2009 and a finalist for the Shaughnessy Cohen Prize for Political Writing. He lives in Toronto with his wife and two children.

ABOUT THE MUNK DEBATES

The Munk Debates are Canada's premier public policy event. Held semi-annually, the debates provide leading thinkers with a global forum to discuss the major public policy issues facing the world and Canada. Each event takes place in Toronto in front of a live audience, and the proceedings are covered by domestic and international media. Participants in recent Munk Debates include Anne Applebaum, Louise Arbour, Stephen K. Bannon, Robert Bell, Tony Blair, John Bolton, Ian Bremmer, Stephen F. Cohen, Daniel Cohn-Bendit, Paul Collier, Howard Dean, Alain de Botton, Alan Dershowitz, Hernando de Soto, E. J. Dionne, Maureen Dowd, Michael Eric Dyson, Gareth Evans, Nigel Farage, Mia Farrow, Niall Ferguson, William Frist, David Frum, Stephen Fry, Newt Gingrich, Malcolm Gladwell, Michelle Goldberg, Jennifer Granholm, David Gratzer, Glenn Greenwald, Stephen Harper, Michael Hayden, Rick Hillier, Christopher Hitchens, Richard

Holbrooke, Laura Ingraham, Josef Joffe, Robert Kagan, Garry Kasparov, Henry Kissinger, Charles Krauthammer, Paul Krugman, Arthur B. Laffer, Lord Nigel Lawson, Stephen Lewis, David Daokui Li, Bjørn Lomborg, Lord Peter Mandelson, Elizabeth May, George Monbiot, Caitlin Moran, Dambisa Moyo, Thomas Mulcair, Vali Nasr, Alexis Ohanian, Camille Paglia, George Papandreou, Jordan Peterson, Steven Pinker, Samantha Power, Vladimir Pozner, Robert Reich, Matt Ridley, David Rosenberg, Hanna Rosin, Simon Schama, Anne-Marie Slaughter, Bret Stephens, Mark Steyn, Kimberley Strassel, Andrew Sullivan, Lawrence Summers, Justin Trudeau, Amos Yadlin, and Fareed Zakaria.

The Munk Debates are a project of the Aurea Foundation, a charitable organization established in 2006 by philanthropists Peter and Melanie Munk to promote public policy research and discussion. For more information, visit www.munkdebates.com.

ABOUT THE INTERVIEWS

Rudyard Griffiths's interviews with H. R. McMaster, Michael Pillsbury, Kishore Mahbubani, and Huiyao Wang were recorded on May 9, 2019. The Aurea Foundation is gratefully acknowledged for permission to reprint excerpts from the following:

(p. 3) "H. R. McMaster in Conversation," by Rudyard Griffiths. Copyright © 2019 Aurea Foundation. Transcribed by Transcript Heroes.

(p. 13) "Michael Pillsbury in Conversation," by Rudyard Griffiths. Copyright © 2019 Aurea Foundation. Transcribed by Transcript Heroes.

(p. 23) "Kishore Mahbubani in Conversation," by Rudyard Griffiths. Copyright © 2019 Aurea Foundation. Transcribed by Transcript Heroes.

The Rise of Populism
Bannon vs. Frum

Throughout the Western world, politics is undergoing a sea change. Long-held notions of the role of government, trade and economic policy, foreign policy, and immigration are being challenged by populist thinkers and movements. Does this surging populist agenda in Western nations signal a permanent shift in our politics? Or is it a passing phenomenon that will remain at the fringes of society and political power? Will our politics continue to be shaped by the postwar consensus on trade, inclusive national identity, and globalization, or by the agenda of insurgent populist politics, parties, and leaders?

The twenty-third semi-annual Munk Debate pits former Donald Trump advisor Stephen K. Bannon against columnist and public intellectual David Frum to debate the future of the liberal political order.

"I want to bring everything crashing down and destroy all of today's establishment."—Stephen K. Bannon

Political Correctness
Dyson and Goldberg vs. Fry and Peterson

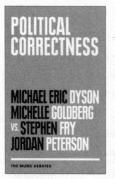

Is political correctness an enemy of free speech, open debate, and the free exchange of ideas? Or, by confronting head-on the dominant power relationships and social norms that exclude marginalized groups, are we creating a more equitable and just society? For some, political correctness is stifling the free and open debate that fuels our democracy. Others insist that creating public spaces and norms that give voice to previously marginalized groups broadens the scope of free speech. The drive toward inclusion over exclusion is essential to creating healthy, diverse societies in an era of rapid social change. Acclaimed journalist, professor, and ordained minister Michael Eric Dyson and *New York Times* columnist Michelle Goldberg are pitted against renowned actor and writer Stephen Fry and University of Toronto professor and author Jordan Peterson to debate the implications of political correctness and freedom of speech.

"Without free speech there is no true thought."—Jordan Peterson

Is American Democracy in Crisis?
Dionne and Sullivan vs. Gingrich and Strassel

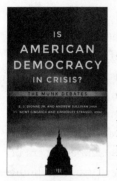

It is the public debate of the moment: Is Donald Trump precipitating a crisis of American democracy? For some the answer is an emphatic "yes." Trump's disregard for the institutions and political norms of U.S. democracy is imperilling the Republic. The sooner his presidency collapses the sooner the healing can begin and the ship of state be righted. For others Trump is not the villain in this drama. Rather, his young presidency is the conduit, not the cause, of America's deep-seated anger toward a privileged and self-dealing Washington elite. Award-winning journalist E. J. Dionne Jr. and influential author and blogger Andrew Sullivan are pitted against former Speaker of the U.S. House of Representatives Newt Gingrich and best-selling author and editor Kimberley Strassel to debate the current crisis of American democracy.

"Our country is now as close to crossing the line from democracy to autocracy as it has been in our lifetimes." —E. J. Dionne Jr.

The Global Refugee Crisis: How Should We Respond?
Arbour and Schama vs. Farage and Steyn

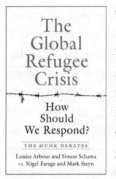

The world is facing the worst humanitarian crisis since the Second World War. Over 300,000 are dead in Syria, and one and a half million are either injured or disabled. Four and a half million people are trying to flee the country. And Syria is just one of a growing number of failed or failing states in the Middle East and North Africa. How should developed nations respond to human suffering on this mass scale? Do the prosperous societies of the West, including Canada and the United States, have a moral imperative to assist as many refugees as they reasonably and responsibly can? Or is this a time for vigilance and restraint in the face of a wave of mass migration that risks upending the tolerance and openness of the West?

"There's nothing to be ashamed of about having an emotional response to the suffering of four million Syrian refugees."
—Simon Schama

houseofanansi.com/collections/munk-debates

Do Humankind's Best Days Lie Ahead?
Pinker and Ridley vs. de Botton and Gladwell

From the Enlightenment onwards, the West has had an enduring belief that through the evolution of institutions, innovations, and ideas, the human condition is improving. But is this the case? Pioneering cognitive scientist Steven Pinker and influential author Matt Ridley take on noted philosopher Alain de Botton and bestselling author Malcolm Gladwell to debate whether humankind's best days lie ahead.

"It's just a brute fact that we don't throw virgins into volcanoes any more. We don't execute people for shoplifting a cabbage. And we used to." —Steven Pinker

Should the West Engage Putin's Russia?
Cohen and Pozner vs. Applebaum and Kasparov

How should the West deal with Vladimir Putin? Acclaimed academic Stephen F. Cohen and veteran journalist and bestselling author Vladimir Pozner square off against internationally renowned expert on Russian history Anne Applebaum and Russian-born political dissident Garry Kasparov to debate the future of the West's relationship with Russia.

"A dictator grows into a monster when he is not confronted at an early stage…And unlike Adolf Hitler, Vladimir Putin has nuclear weapons."—Garry Kasparov

Does State Spying Make Us Safer?
Hayden and Dershowitz vs. Greenwald and Ohanian

In a risk-filled world, democracies are increasingly turning to large-scale state surveillance, at home and abroad, to fight complex and unconventional threats. Former head of the CIA and NSA Michael Hayden and civil liberties lawyer Alan Dershowitz square off against journalist Glenn Greenwald and reddit co-founder Alexis Ohanian to debate if the government should be able to monitor our activities in order to keep us safe.

"Surveillance equals power. The more you know about someone, the more you can control and manipulate them in all sorts of ways." — Glenn Greenwald

Are Men Obsolete?
Rosin and Dowd vs. Moran and Paglia

For the first time in history, will it be better to be a woman than a man in the upcoming century? Renowned author and editor Hanna Rosin and Pulitzer Prize–winning columnist Maureen Dowd challenge *New York Times*–best-selling author Caitlin Moran and trail-blazing social critic Camille Paglia to debate the relative decline of the power and status of men in the workplace, the family, and society at large.

"Feminism was always wrong to pretend women could 'have it all.' It is not male society but Mother Nature who lays the heaviest burden on women."—Camille Paglia

North America's Lost Decade?
Krugman and Rosenberg vs. Summers and Bremmer

The future of the North American economy is more uncertain than ever. In this edition of the Munk Debates, Nobel Prize–winning economist Paul Krugman and chief economist and strategist at Gluskin Sheff + Associates David Rosenberg square off against former U.S. treasury secretary Lawrence Summers and bestselling author Ian Bremmer to tackle the resolution, "Be it resolved: North America faces a Japan-style era of high unemployment and slow growth."

"It's now impossible to deny the obvious, which is that we are not now, and have never been, on the road to recovery." — Paul Krugman

READ MORE FROM THE MUNK DEBATES—
CANADA'S PREMIER DEBATE SERIES

Does the 21st Century Belong to China?
Kissinger and Zakaria vs. Ferguson and Li

Is China's rise unstoppable? Former U.S. secretary of state Henry Kissinger and CNN's Fareed Zakaria pair off against leading historian Niall Ferguson and world-renowned Chinese economist David Daokui Li to debate China's emergence as a global force—the key geopolitical issue of our time.

This edition of the Munk Debates also features the first formal public debate Dr. Kissinger has participated in on China's future.

"I have enormous difficulty imagining a world dominated by China...I believe the concept that any one country will domi-nate the world is, in itself, a misunderstanding of the world in which we live now."—Henry Kissinger

houseofanansi.com/collections/munk-debates

Hitchens vs. Blair
Christopher Hitchens vs. Tony Blair

Intellectual juggernaut and staunch atheist Christopher Hitchens goes head-to-head with former British prime minister Tony Blair, one of the Western world's most openly devout political leaders, on the age-old question: Is religion a force for good in the world? Few world leaders have had a greater hand in shaping current events than Blair; few writers have been more outspoken and polarizing than Hitchens.

Sharp, provocative, and thoroughly engrossing, *Hitchens vs. Blair* is a rigorous and electrifying intellectual sparring match on the contentious questions that continue to dog the topic of religion in our globalized world.

"If religious instruction were not allowed until the child had attained the age of reason, we would be living in a very different world."— Christopher Hitchens

READ MORE FROM THE MUNK DEBATES—
CANADA'S PREMIER DEBATE SERIES

The Munk Debates: Volume One
Edited by Rudyard Griffiths
Introduction by Peter Munk

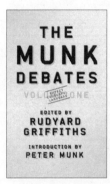

Launched in 2008 by philanthropists Peter and Melanie Munk, the Munk Debates is Canada's premier international debate series, a highly anticipated cultural event that brings together the world's brightest minds.

This volume includes the first five debates in the series and features twenty leading thinkers and doers arguing for or against provocative resolutions that address pressing public policy concerns such as the future of global security, the implications of humanitarian intervention, the effectiveness of foreign aid, the threat of climate change, and the state of health care in Canada and the United States.

"By trying to highlight the most important issues at crucial moments in the global conversation, these debates not only profile the ideas and solutions of some of our brightest thinkers and doers, but crystallize public passion and knowledge, helping to tackle some global challenges confronting humankind."
—Peter Munk

houseofanansi.com/collections/munk-debates